Using
Microsoft Office™
to
Enhance Student Learning

To Charlene, Trey, Chris, and Ethan—the source of my
inspiration, motivation, and perspiration.
I love you guys.

Using
Microsoft Office™
to
Enhance Student Learning

Allan F. Livers, Jr.

CORWIN PRESS
A SAGE Publications Company
Thousand Oaks, CA 91320

Note: All screen shots are reprinted by permission of Microsoft Corporation

Microsoft Office is a registered trademark of Microsoft Corporation in the United States and/or other countries. All brand names and product names used in this book are trade names, service marks, trademarks, or registered trademarks of their respective owners. The author is not associated with Microsoft or any other product or vendor mentioned in this book.

All terms mentioned in this book that are known to be trademarks have been appropriately capitalized. Rather than list all the names and entities that own the trademarks or insert a trademarked name, the author and publisher state that they are using the names only for editorial purposes and to the benefit of the trademark owner with no intention of infringing upon that mark.

The author has attempted to include trademark information for screen shots, icons, clip art, and Office Assistants referred to in this book. Although the author has made reasonable efforts in gathering this information, he cannot guarantee its accuracy.

For information:

Corwin Press
A SAGE Company
2455 Teller Road
Thousand Oaks, California 91320
www.corwinpress.com

SAGE Ltd.
1 Oliver's Yard
55 City Road
London EC1Y 1SP
United Kingdom

SAGE India Pvt. Ltd.
B 1/I 1 Mohan Cooperative Industrial Area
Mathura Road, New Delhi 110 044
India

SAGE Asia-Pacific Pte. Ltd.
33 Pekin Street #02-01
Far East Square
Singapore 048763

Printed in the United States of America.

Library of Congress Cataloging-in-Publication Data

Livers, Allan F.
Using Microsoft Office to enhance student learning / by Allan F. Livers.
    p. cm.
ISBN 978-1-4129-4121-1 (cloth w/cd)
ISBN 978-1-4129-4122-8 (paper w/cd)
   1. Computer managed instruction. 2. Computer-assisted instruction.
3. Teaching—Aids and devices. 4. Microsoft Office. I. Title.

LB1028.46.L58 2008
371.33'4—dc22   2007020451

This book is printed on acid-free paper.

07 08 09 10 11   10 9 8 7 6 5 4 3 2 1

Acquisitions Editor:	Elizabeth Brenkus
Editorial Assistants:	Desirée Enayati, Ena Rosen
Production Editor:	Veronica Stapleton
Copy Editor:	Linda Gray
Typesetter:	C&M Digitals (P) Ltd.
Proofreader:	Dorothy Hoffman
Indexer:	Molly Hall
Cover Designer:	Lisa Miller

Contents

List of Illustrations and Figures

Chapter 4: Microsoft Excel Projects

Preface

With the current emphasis on standards-based testing and teacher accountability for student performance, educators are under increased pressure to help their students succeed academically. Technology, while not meant to be a panacea, has been shown to help in some cases when properly applied. Computers, although now found in almost every classroom in the country, are still not being used effectively in many cases. It seems that every July, teachers attend inservice training on the latest and greatest reading program or math program that is supposed to show phenomenal improvements in student achievement. Many of these may be computer based. Then, for some unexplained reason, these phenomenal improvements do not occur, teachers and parents may become jaded, and we roll out yet another reading or math program the following July.

The purpose of this book is not to promote a particular new software package, requiring investment of scarce educational dollars and long hours spent learning the new system. Instead, this book will show you some ideas for using to better advantage a set of software packages that already comes standard on most school-based computers in the nation—Microsoft (MS) Office 2003 for PC, specifically Microsoft Word, Microsoft PowerPoint, Microsoft Excel, Microsoft Access, and Microsoft Publisher.

Even though these projects were created using Microsoft Office 2003, users with older versions of Microsoft Office will still find this publication a useful source of ideas and inspiration. While the basic layout of the screens has changed between Microsoft Office 2003 and the older versions, you can still create equivalent projects using the earlier programs. To allow access to users who do not have Microsoft Office 2003 installed, an additional file on the companion CD has many of the projects saved in older versions of Office. And while the instructions herein are designed for PC users, the MAC user who has experience with Microsoft Office products may find this book particularly useful as well. The Microsoft Publisher projects are not available in versions older than 2003.

The projects could have been ordered in several different ways (by grade level, by content area, by preferred learning modality, software package, or difficulty level.) The heart of this book lies in the project descriptions, grouped by software type, with individual chapters on using Word, PowerPoint, Excel, Access, and Publisher. Publisher is placed at the end of this list since only users with Office 2003 will be able to use this. Those with pre-2003 software will need to stay with projects in the first four categories. Within each chapter, the projects are further ordered according to difficulty level. The easier projects are described first, with the more challenging projects listed at the end of each chapter. The first part of each project contains classification icons so the reader can readily find projects of specific interest. Additionally, an Access database on the companion CD has a breakdown of each project in the book. This data can be sorted as desired for those who are looking for very specific project groups (i.e., only science projects, or only elementary school projects).

The user of this book with only a beginner-level familiarity with Microsoft Office products would do well to simply use the sample projects on the enclosed companion CD and modify as needed for classroom use. For these individuals, it may be best to view this book not so much as a tutorial guide but, rather, as a "how-to-use-the-templates" guide. Those users who have a slightly higher, or intermediate-level, familiarity with these programs will be able to design these projects from scratch, either by following the directions included with the projects, or by reverse engineering the sample projects on the companion CD. Either way, it is not necessary to be an advanced-level user to take full advantage of this resource.

This book will prove useful to several different groups of individuals:

- General education public school K–12 teachers will be encouraged as they learn ways to increase student achievement in the classrooms.
- Classroom teachers will be able to use the technology currently available in many classrooms to help them achieve state-mandated curriculum and learning standards.
- Likewise, special education teachers will find this book useful as they look for ways to reach and teach students with special needs.
- School computer resource teachers tasked with using and maintaining the school computers will also find many useful projects here that can be used to meet educational and technology objectives and help students master content area learning standards.
- School administrators will be able to schedule inservice training sessions for their faculties in techniques designed to improve student performance. Those administrators looking for tools to improve student performance on standardized tests will find many aids to instruction that can help.
- College and university professors in schools of education and teacher preparatory programs should read this book and encourage student teacher candidates to get a copy for use in the classroom.
- Individual practitioners can use this as a classroom resource during lesson planning and scope and sequence development.
- Workshop facilitators can use this to train attendees in better ways to teach their students.
- Additionally, parents and others interested in home schooling will find dozens of useful activities to reinforce instruction.

Several enhancements set this book apart from others currently available. Each project description includes possible uses of the project by grade level and content area. Additionally, it contains approximately 100 screenshots, illustrative of finished projects, along with recommended Web sites for further information about the project.

Six major chapters and various supporting resources make up this book. Major chapters include:

- Chapter 1: Introduction to Using Microsoft Office to Enhance Student Learning
  - Intro to the book and to how technology can be used in classrooms to help meet state-mandated educational standards

- Chapter 2: Microsoft Word Projects
  - o Directions for completing 20 Microsoft Word projects
- Chapter 3: Microsoft PowerPoint Projects
  - o Directions for completing 20 Microsoft PowerPoint projects
- Chapter 4: Microsoft Excel Projects
  - o Directions for completing 13 Microsoft Excel projects
- Chapter 5: Microsoft Access Projects
  - o Directions for completing 14 Microsoft Access projects
- Chapter 6: Microsoft Publisher Projects
  - o Directions for completing 20 Microsoft Publisher Projects

The companion CD, created using Microsoft Office 2003, contains four resources. The first (Resource A) is a collection of ready-to-use templates for 75% of the projects described in the book. While most of the project pages will describe how to create the desired resource, in many cases it may prove easier to simply adapt the template for classroom use. Additionally, as mentioned earlier, the companion CD has many of these projects saved in an older format for users with pre-2003 editions of Microsoft Office.

Resource B, a Microsoft Access database, allows the projects to be sorted according to the desired characteristic, including software used, suggested grade level, content area, or level of difficulty, to name a few. This feature will prove useful for teachers looking for projects that may be well suited to a specific group of students.

Effective lessons have clearly defined goals and objectives. The states are very specific in determining what must be taught in state-funded public schools. While the terms may vary from state to state, generally states will identify what you are expected to teach in public schools. Be they learning standards, curriculum standards, instructional standards, or performance standards, these objectives are already determined for every state in the Union. These standards are generally available on state Department of Education Web sites. The table in Resource C lists the Web addresses for the 50 state Departments of Education and corresponding pages containing required state curriculum and instructional standards. This table on the companion CD allows hyperlink access directly to the desired site. By using these state Web sites, you can be assured that you are teaching to the most current state educational standards available for your particular area.

The final resource on the companion CD (Resource D) is a collection of the supplemental information Web sites identified at the end of many of the individual projects. These sites contain additional suggestions on how to develop or use the associated projects.

Acknowledgments

With any project of this magnitude there are, of course, many people without whose contribution this book would never have come about. My dad, Al Livers, Sr., a newspaper reporter for much of his life, engendered a love for the written word in my sisters Pennie, Freddie, and Supey and in my mother Marjie, all authors in their own right, and he has had no less an influence on my own aspirations.

I first became interested in authoring a book when I met my first real live author, Judith Bardwick, a professor at San Diego State University. Judy's passion for writing and life were equally infectious, and I have always valued her counsel.

James Stronge, my dissertation committee chairman, had already authored and edited several books when I served as his graduate assistant at The College of William & Mary. Working with him on several projects, I was able to observe portions of the authorship process firsthand.

A special thanks to my good friend, Mr. Sheridan Barber, an absolute whiz at working with Microsoft Office in general and Access in particular. His help and suggestions transformed several mediocre projects into outstanding ones.

I would also like to thank the six individuals who performed blind peer reviews of the manuscript. Your comments and insight helped identify several improvements that were incorporated before going to print. Unfortunately, since it was a blind review, I don't know who you are, but thanks anyway.

Thanks also to Lizzie Brenkus, Acquisitions Editor at Corwin Press, and her Editorial Assistants Desirée Enayati and Ena Rosen. Were it not for their outstanding technical support and "gentle encouragement" when I was late meeting a deadline or submitting a draft (or two), this project might never have been completed. Thanks go to Lisa Miller for creating a dynamite cover design that truly captures the essence of this book and to Linda Gray for her meticulous attention to detail as my copy editor. I would also like to thank my Production Editor, Veronica Stapleton and Media Editor, Peggie Howard, whose meticulous attention to detail proved instrumental in the final weeks of the publication process.

Thanks also to friends and colleagues Jeanne Blevins, Daniel Cooper, Joanne Hardesty, Donna Hindlin, Dusty Howell, Lisa Vernon-Dotson, Jim Waldman, and Charlotte Worley for their support and encouragement along the way.

Finally, I want to especially thank the many teachers, students, and others who have devised countless ways to use Microsoft Office to enhance student learning and from whose ideas I have freely drawn for inspiration in the drafting of this book.

If you find some particularly engaging projects in these pages, I would love to hear from you. Or if you have projects of your own that you use to enhance student learning, shoot me an e-mail and tell me about it. I can be contacted at blivers2@juno.com.

Corwin Press gratefully acknowledges the contributions of the following individuals:

Sara Armstrong, Director
Sara Armstrong Consulting
Berkeley, CA

Sara Dexter, Assistant Professor
University of Virginia
Charlottesville, VA

Jeremy Duntley, National Board Certified Teacher
Pittsfield Middle School
Pittsford, NY

Theresa M. Dyson, Computer Resource Specialist
Hermitage Elementary School
Virginia Beach, VA

Jeanine Heil, Director of Instruction, Technology, and Curriculum
Eastampton School District
Eastampton, NJ

Dusti Howell, Associate Professor
Emporia State University
Emporia, KS

Joseph Meersman, Video Production Teacher
Toppenish High School
Toppenish, WA

Kenneth W. Smead, Computer Resource Specialist
Larkspur Middle School
Virginia Beach, VA

Gayle Wuesthoff, Computer Resource Specialist
King's Grant Elementary School
Virginia Beach, VA

Mark Westerfield, Distance Learning Coordinator
White River School District
Buckley, WA

About the Author

Allan F. (Bud) Livers, Jr., PhD, currently serves as the Learning Standards Officer at the Center for Naval Intelligence in Virginia Beach, Virginia. Additionally, he serves as Senior Faculty for Cambridge College, Chesapeake Virginia Campus, in the Masters in Education, Special Education program. His interest in media and technology in the classroom was initially cultivated in his job as a special education teacher, working with students with an emotional disturbance at a regional public day school, where he sought new and improved ways to teach students with disabilities. He went on to teach the media and technology classes as an Assistant Professor in the Department of Teacher Education at Chowan University in North Carolina. He has also worked as the developer and supervisor of the Jails Education Program in Virginia Beach, Virginia, tasked with providing special education services for incarcerated youth and young adults in the city jail. Bud received his PhD in Educational Planning, Policy, and Leadership, with emphasis in Special Education Administration from The College of William & Mary, in Williamsburg, Virginia. He received his MSEd in elementary education with endorsement in special education from Old Dominion University in Norfolk, Virginia. Bud's research interests include stress and burnout in the classroom, and he has presented his "Lighter Side of Teacher Burnout" to state, national, and international audiences. Bud is a retired Naval Officer who served as a Surface Warfare Officer during Operation Desert Storm in the Persian Gulf. He lives with his wife and three sons in Virginia Beach, Virginia.

1

Introduction to Using Microsoft Office to Enhance Student Learning

American Schools are experiencing a technological revolution. Computers, LCD projectors, smart boards, and wireless Internet connections, once found in only the most elite schools, are now becoming as much a mainstay in school buildings as the cafeteria. This influx of technology is found not only in computer labs but in individual classrooms as well. They are becoming increasingly wired for the Internet and personal computers. Yet despite this influx of capital and technology, many school computers are underused, relegated to housing a few educational games and perhaps to some minor record-keeping functions.

Standards-based reform and accountability continue to take on increased importance. Given the recent pressure to meet state-mandated curriculum standards, many teachers believe they don't have the time to spend on computer projects beyond those required to teach to the basic technology standards. Schools are required to meet challenging content and academic standards as set by state boards of education. Computers, properly used, can help achieve students' state-mandated educational standards.

Many classrooms suffer, not from a lack of technology but from a lack of understanding how best to use the technology already in place. This book is designed to help teachers meet the demands of high-stakes curriculum standards using technology hardware and the Microsoft Office software available in most classrooms. The book contains over 80 practical and interesting projects designed to help teachers teach to the state learning standards. These projects are described, step-by-step, along with recommendations for classroom use by elementary, middle, and high school teachers in content areas of language arts, math, science, and social studies.

This book is not designed as a primer on Microsoft Office products. That information is available elsewhere and written about in exacting detail by other authors. The reader of this book will be expected to already have a working knowledge of Microsoft Office products, to include Word, PowerPoint, Excel, Access, and Publisher. It is not intended that this book teach the "nuts and bolts" of these programs but, rather, that teachers may learn new ways to use these programs in helping their students master the curriculum objectives. In addition, the extensive collection of templates found on the companion CD that accompanies this text will make it easy for even the novice user to adapt these projects for classroom use. The examples cited and the screenshots included in this text are from Microsoft Office 2003, but most of these projects can be adapted for use on older versions as well.

Project Format

Each project has a standard format, with sections common to all projects in the book. This way you can readily locate applicable parts of each project. Common sections in each project include the following:

Project title: Generally, you should be able to determine the nature of the project from its title.

Project number: Each project has a distinct number. The software used for the project can be determined from the first letters in the project number, as follows:

WD = Microsoft Word

PP = Microsoft PowerPoint

XL = Microsoft Excel

AC = Microsoft Access

PL = Microsoft Publisher

Degree of difficulty: A five-pointed star icon will indicate the degree of project difficulty. The more shaded points on the star, the more challenging the project will be.

Software used: This section is a backup way to tell what software is used in the creation of the project.

Additional hardware: If the project requires a scanner or a printer hookup, it will be indicated in this section.

Internet connection required: Some projects will require an Internet connection. If so, it will be indicated here.

Template available: The companion CD that accompanies this book contains templates for most of the projects. These templates will prove to be a real time-saver, especially on the more challenging projects.

Created by: Some of these projects are designed to be teacher created. Some are student created, and some projects may be either student or teacher created.

Project type: This section will tell you if the project is primarily designed to support classroom instruction or classroom administration. Some projects can be used for both.

Student learning style: While it is acknowledged that most of these projects work well with the visual learner, the aural and kinesthetic learners can gain much from these projects as well.

Approximate time: This section gives a rough estimate of the length of time required to create the project. Projects may take anywhere from just a few minutes, to several hours to complete. Use this section when planning how many class sessions to devote to the project.

Grade level: This section lists the general grade level areas best served by the project. While not exclusively confined to these grade levels, generally, the projects may be best used in elementary school, middle school, or high school as indicated here.

Content area: Here you will find suggested content areas for which the project may be well suited. Choices include language arts, math, science, and social studies.

Comments: This section will contain some general information about the project, along with some possible suggestions for use.

Procedures: In this section, you will find the step-by-step instructions necessary to complete the project.

Figures: Screenshots of actual projects are found here. Most of these screenshots come from projects or templates included on the companion CD.

For more information: This section will usually contain the URL of a Web address to go to for additional information on the topic addressed in the project.

Icons

Each project contains several icons to help identify important information about each of the projects. Icons used in this book include the following:

Level of difficulty: These icons indicate approximate degree of difficulty in creating the indicated project. In several cases, projects that may be rather challenging to create from scratch have been indicated as fairly easy because you are encouraged to use the template provided on the companion CD.

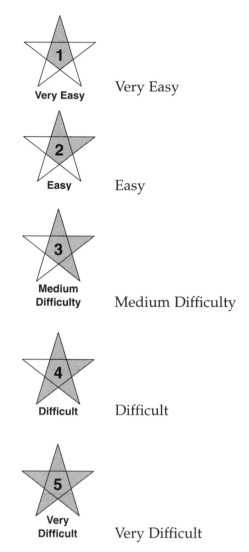

Very Easy

Easy

Medium Difficulty

Difficult

Very Difficult

Created by: Icons in this section indicate who might best create the indicated project. Most of these projects can be either teacher or student created, depending on intended use.

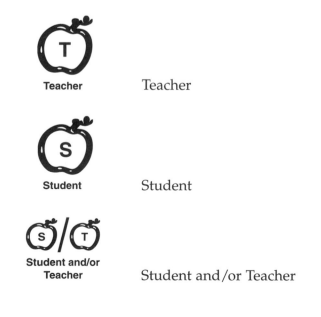

Teacher

Student

Student and/or Teacher

Project type: These icons indicate if the project is primarily intended to support classroom instruction or if it is better suited to support classroom administration and management.

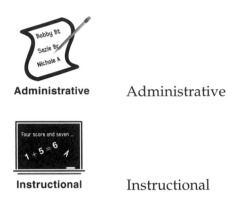

Administrative Administrative

Instructional Instructional

Learning style: While most of these projects primarily support a visual learning style, several of these can be used to support aural and kinesthetic learners as well.

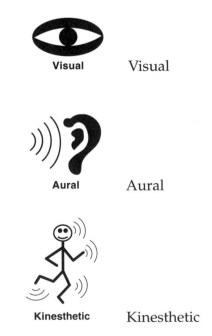

Visual Visual

Aural Aural

Kinesthetic Kinesthetic

Content area: Icons in this section indicate for which of the content areas the project might be well suited. Content area teachers may find it useful to sort the projects according to supported content to help in selecting projects.

 Language Arts

 Math

 Science

 Social Studies

 N/A

SAMPLE PROJECT PAGE

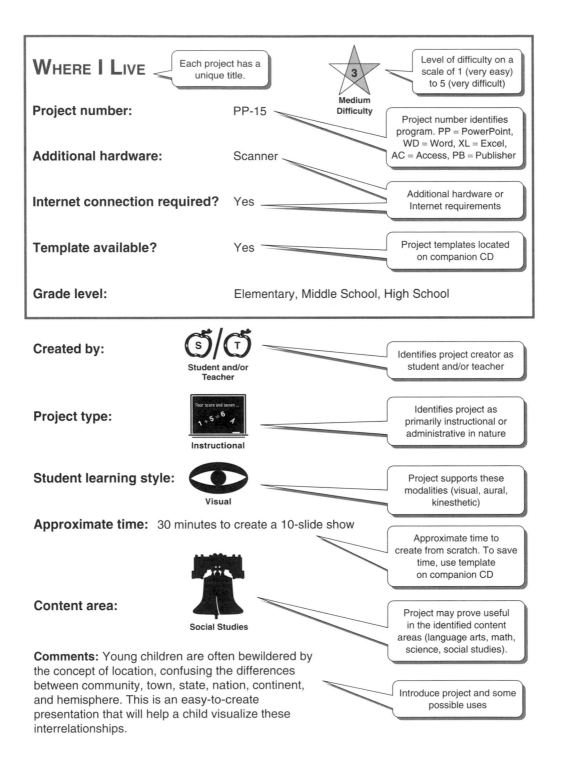

WHERE I LIVE — Each project has a unique title.

3 Medium Difficulty — Level of difficulty on a scale of 1 (very easy) to 5 (very difficult)

Project number: PP-15 — Project number identifies program. PP = PowerPoint, WD = Word, XL = Excel, AC = Access, PB = Publisher

Additional hardware: Scanner

Internet connection required? Yes — Additional hardware or Internet requirements

Template available? Yes — Project templates located on companion CD

Grade level: Elementary, Middle School, High School

Created by: Student and/or Teacher — Identifies project creator as student and/or teacher

Project type: Instructional — Identifies project as primarily instructional or administrative in nature

Student learning style: Visual — Project supports these modalities (visual, aural, kinesthetic)

Approximate time: 30 minutes to create a 10-slide show — Approximate time to create from scratch. To save time, use template on companion CD

Content area: Social Studies — Project may prove useful in the identified content areas (language arts, math, science, social studies).

Comments: Young children are often bewildered by the concept of location, confusing the differences between community, town, state, nation, continent, and hemisphere. This is an easy-to-create presentation that will help a child visualize these interrelationships. — Introduce project and some possible uses

Procedures: ──────

> Directions for creating the project.

1. Open a new Microsoft PowerPoint presentation.

2. Select **Title Slide** and enter name of presentation and class information.

> **Bold text** indicates where you should click

3. Select a new **Title and Content** slide. Make five copies of this slide.

4. On the title line of these five slides, place the words "My Neighborhood," "My Town" (or city), "My State," "My Country," "My Continent," "My Hemisphere," and "My World," respectively.

5. In the content area of each slide, place an image of the appropriate area. These images can be scanned pictures or images downloaded from the Internet and placed in a picture file created for this purpose. Use a star symbol to indicate the student's home on each map.

6. Your final presentation may include slides that look something like this:

> This area contains screen shots of the finished project

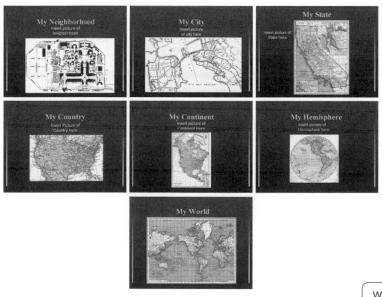

> Where to go for additional help & information

For more information online: www.mapquest.com

COMPANION CD

This book comes with a companion CD containing resources that will prove valuable as you use these projects in your classroom.

Resource A: Complete Projects Database

Resource A is an Access database containing information about all the projects in this book. Use this database as you look for ideas. To search for a certain category of projects—say, for example, all math projects or all elementary-level projects—open the "Media & Tech Projects" table, then select **Records > Sort > Advanced Filter/Sort** from the drop-down menu at the top of the screen. Select the desired sorting criteria, select **Ascending** or **Descending** order, then **Apply Filter/Sort**. In this way, you can immediately identify projects that might be most appropriate for your chosen subject or grade level.

In the "Grade Lvl" column on the Media & Tech Projects table, "E" stands for elementary school, "M" for middle school, and "H" is for high school. In the "Content" column, "L/A" stands for language arts, "M" is for math, "S" is for science, and "S/S" stands for social studies.

Resource B: Project Templates

In Resource B, you will find the many templates and project aids that correspond to the written directions. Not all the projects have a corresponding project listed here; others may have more than one. They are numbered using the same title found in the basic project description, only the file extensions may have changed. For example, the template for Project PP-01, Water Cycle, will be listed as "PP-01 Water Cycle.ppt." For some projects, there may be two related templates. For example, a math worksheet project may have one template with blank spaces for students to fill in and a second template may have the correct answers already entered for the teacher's use.

Resource C: State Departments of Education and Curriculum Standards Web Sites

The next item, Resource C, is a table listing the URLs of the 50 state Departments of Education Web site home pages, along with the pages for the state academic standards. When your computer is connected to the Internet, these URLs are designed to hyperlink you directly to the desired site. For better projects, identify the required academic standards you plan to teach in the lesson ahead of time. Select and design your projects accordingly to ensure that your instruction is aligned with your state's curriculum standards. Note: These Web sites were valid at the time of publication; however, some links may no longer work because pages change frequently. If the state Curriculum Standards page has moved, go to the state DOE Web site and follow the links from there to the Curriculum Standards.

Resource D: Project Supplemental Information Web Sites

Many of the project descriptions in this book end with a Web site address where you may find additional information pertaining to that particular project. These addresses are also included in Resource D, a Word document with a hyperlink to the respective Web site. By using this table, you eliminate the need to manually enter the URL into your Web browser and you can quickly access the desired site.

FAIR USE OF COPYRIGHT MATERIAL

Several of the projects may require you to copy portions of works protected by copyright. Please note the Fair Use of Copyright Material below prior to using any copyright material in your projects.

Fair Use Laws and Plagiarism

Fair Use

The following information was taken from the U.S. Copyright Office Web site http://www.copyright.gov/fls/fl102.html

One of the rights accorded to the owner of copyright is the right to reproduce or to authorize others to reproduce the work in copies or phonorecords. This right is subject to certain limitations found in sections 107 through 118 of the Copyright Act (title 17, U. S. Code). One of the more important limitations is the doctrine of "fair use." Although fair use was not mentioned in the previous copyright law, the doctrine has developed through a substantial number of court decisions over the years. This doctrine has been codified in section 107 of the copyright law.

Section 107 contains a list of the various purposes for which the reproduction of a particular work may be considered "fair," such as criticism, comment, news reporting, teaching, scholarship, and research. Section 107 also sets out four factors to be considered in determining whether or not a particular use is fair:

1. the purpose and character of the use, including whether such use is of commercial nature or is for nonprofit educational purposes;

2. the nature of the copyrighted work;

3. amount and substantiality of the portion used in relation to the copyrighted work as a whole; and

4. the effect of the use upon the potential market for or value of the copyrighted work.

The distinction between "fair use" and infringement may be unclear and not easily defined. There is no specific number of words, lines, or notes that may safely be taken without permission. Acknowledging the source of the copyrighted material does not substitute for obtaining permission.

Plagiarism

Readers are urged to avoid plagiarism when creating these projects. Wikipedia Encyclopedia (http://en.wikipedia.org/wiki/Plagiarism) defines plagiarism as: *"the study of 'honestly' claiming or implying original authorship of material which has not actually been created, such as when a person incorporates material from someone else's work into his own work without attributing it. Within academia, plagiarism is seen as academic dishonesty and is a serious and punishable academic offense. Plagiarism may happen unintentionally in the case of unconscious plagiarism or if a plagiarist is unaware of the need for citation. Unintentional plagiarism is not dishonest but it may be careless."*

2

Microsoft Word Projects

In this chapter you will find the following activities:

Project Number	Title	Difficulty	Created By
WD-01	True/False Test	1	Teacher
WD-02	Multiple-Choice Test	2	Teacher
WD-03	Essay Test	2	Teacher
WD-04	Mixed-Design Test	2	Teacher
WD-05	Scavenger Hunt	2	Student and/or Teacher
WD-06	Grade-Level Readability Test	2	Teacher
WD-07	Charts and Graphs	2	Student and/or Teacher
WD-08	Daily Journal	2	Student
WD-09	Creating Templates	3	Teacher
WD-10	Math Templates	3	Teacher
WD-11	Class Newsletter	3	Student and/or Teacher
WD-12	Cloze Test	3	Teacher
WD-13	Maze Test	3	Teacher
WD-14	Peer Editing and Reviewer Comments	3	Student and/or Teacher
WD-15	Decision-Making Aid	3	Teacher
WD-16	Memorizing Text Passages	3	Teacher
WD-17	Flash Cards	3	Student and/or Teacher
WD-18	Course Syllabus	3	Teacher
WD-19	Writing Guide	3	Teacher
WD-20	How to Write Instructions	3	Teacher

INTRODUCTION TO MICROSOFT WORD

Microsoft Word is perhaps one of the world's best-known word processing programs. With Word, you will be able to design, edit, and print text documents that you or your students have created. Microsoft Word may be confused with Microsoft Works, a somewhat less capable word processing program that often comes already installed on many computers at time of purchase. Chances are your school division has already upgraded to the more capable program, Microsoft Word. Computers with Microsoft Works installed will often times not be able to read documents designed in Microsoft Word and vice versa, despite their both being Microsoft products. Another popular word processing program, Word Perfect, is licensed by a different company. Microsoft Word is not able to open documents created in Word Perfect. If you really need the document to be readable by both Microsoft Word and Word Perfect, try saving your document in rich text format—that is, with an ".rtf" extension—and you can read it using either program.

Microsoft Word has quickly become the program of choice in many classrooms. With a variety of text options, Word can be used to design tests, lesson plans, essays, correspondence, note-taking guides, permission slips, and many other routine classroom tasks. Reviewing functions allow you to electronically review and comment on written assignments. Mail merge functions can help as you send home correspondence to parents or students.

TRUE/FALSE TEST

1

Very Easy

Project Number: WD-01

Additional hardware: None

Internet connection required? No

Template available? Yes

Grade Level: Elementary, Middle School, High School

Created by:

Teacher

Project type:

Administrative

Student learning style:

Visual

Approximate time: 10 minutes to create a 12-question test

Content Area:

Language Arts

Math

Science

Social Studies

Comments: Easy to administer and grade, the true/false test is one of the more popular assessment tools available. This test is useful as a quick assessment device. While it may not test for depth of knowledge in a particular area, it can provide a quick overview of the student's general understanding of the subject matter.

Procedures: You may insert your information on the template provided on the companion CD, or you may choose to follow the procedures below.

1. Open a new document in Microsoft Word.

2. Type the identifying information at the top of the page, listing the course name and the test title, and allowing space for the student name and date.

3. Add directions to the student, if any. For example, "Answer each question True or False," or "Circle T or F for each of the following questions."

4. Precede each question with either a space to write the answer, or with a "T/F" for the student to circle.

5. Write the questions or statements.

Type the name of your test here

Instructor: Type your name here _____   Name: _____
                                                   Class: _____
                                                   Period: _____
                                                   Date: _____

Type the test instructions here. For example, instruct the student to read each question carefully, then write T (true) or F (false) on the line next to the question.

  1. _____Type the question here.
  2. _____Type the question here.
  3. _____Type the question here.
  4. _____Type the question here.
  5. _____Type the question here.
  6. _____Type the question here.
  7. _____Type the question here.
  8. _____Type the question here.
  9. _____Type the question here.
 10. _____Type the question here.
 11. _____Type the question here.
 12. _____Type the question here.

For more information online, go to:

www.microsoftoffice.com

MULTIPLE-CHOICE TEST

Project Number: WD-02

Additional hardware: None

Internet connection required? No

Template available? Yes

Grade Level: Elementary, Middle School, High School

2 Easy

Created by:

Teacher

Project type:

Administrative

Student learning style:

Visual

Approximate time: 30 minutes to create a 10-question test

Content Area:

Language Arts

Math

Science

Social Studies

Comments: The multiple-choice test is by far one of the most popular tests in use today. As this format is used in most state-mandated end-of-grade standardized tests, it is good to expose your students to this testing style often and in varied ways.

The multiple-choice text consists of two parts: (a) the question (known as the "stem") and (b) the possible responses, containing both incorrect answers (known as "distracters") and the correct response (the "answer"). Easy to grade, the multiple-choice test is a perennial favorite among teachers and educators everywhere. This widely used assessment device can be created easily using the template on the companion CD. If you do not have access to the companion CD, you may either download a template from the Microsoft Office Web site, or you may create your own three-choice test from scratch. The Chicago Public Schools Web site listed below has some excellent guidance on writing better multiple-choice tests. Check it out before writing your questions.

Procedures: You may insert your information on the template provided on the companion CD, or you may choose to follow the procedures below.

1. Open a new document in Microsoft Word.

2. Type the identifying information at the top of the page, listing the course name and the test title, and allowing space for the student name and date.

3. Add directions to the student, if any. For example, "Read each question carefully, and select the best answer from those listed. Print the letter of the correct answer next to the question."

4. Type the question. Precede each question with an identifying number, followed by a blank space for recording the answer.

5. List the possible answers below each question. Precede each possible answer with an identifying letter.

Type the name of your test here

Instructor: Type your name here   Name: _____

Class: _____

Period: _____

Date: _____

Type the test instructions here. For example, instruct the student to read each question carefully, then print the letter of the correct answer on the line next to the question.

1. _____ Type the first question here
   a. First answer
   b. Second answer
   c. Third Answer

2. _____ Type the second question here
   a. First answer
   b. Second answer
   c. Third Answer

3. _____ Type the third question here
   a. First answer
   b. Second answer
   c. Third Answer

4. _____ Type the fourth question here
   a. First answer
   b. Second answer
   c. Third Answer

For more information online, go to:

Chicago Public Schools Web site:

http://intranet.cps.k12.il.us/Assessments/Preparation/HS_Standardized_Test_Prep/HS_Appendix/HS_APX_Tips_for_Creating_Multi/hs_apx_tips_for_creating_multi.html

Microsoft Office Website:

http://office.microsoft.com/en-us/templates/FX100595491033.aspx

ESSAY TEST

Project Number: WD-03

Additional hardware: None

Internet connection required? No

Template available? No

Grade Level: Elementary, Middle School, High School

2 Easy

Created by:
Teacher

Project type:
Administrative

Student learning style:
Visual

Approximate time: 30 minutes to create a 10-question test

Content Area:
Language Arts

Math

Science

Social Studies

Comments: Essay tests are a valuable means of assessing student understanding and mastery of learning objectives. They naturally allow for more creativity in answering and give teachers greater flexibility in grading as well. This is a particularly useful tool for evaluating students with special education needs. By having your students take their essay tests on the computer, you can concentrate more on the gist of the students' answers rather than the distractions of poor handwriting and minor misspellings.

Procedures:

1. Open a new Microsoft Word document.

2. Select **View > Toolbars > Forms.**

3. Enter headings for Name, Date, and Subject at the top of the page. Next to each of these headings, open the **Form** toolbar and enter select **Text Form Field**.

4. Click on the **Text Form Field** you just added next to **Subject.**

5. On the **Forms** toolbar, select **Form Field Options.**

6. In the space **Default Text**, enter the words **Insert Subject Here**. Enter. (This will identify the space where you are to enter the SUBJECT when writing the test.)

7. Designate a space for the test directions by entering the word **Directions**, followed by a **Text Form Field** from the **Forms** toolbar.

8. List the numbers 1 through 5 equally spaced down the left side of the page (or however many questions you want to include in your test). After each number, place a **Text Form Field** from the **Forms** toolbar. In each of these, select the **Form Field Options** button from the **Forms** toolbar. Type the words "Insert Question 1 in this place," changing the question number as needed.

9. You may want to provide a space to designate the point value of each question. To do this after each "Insert question . . . " entry, place **Text Form Field** and **Points.**

Type the name of your test here

Instructor: Type your name here

Name: _____
Class: _____
Period: _____
Date: _____

Type test directions here. For example, instruct the student to read each question carefully, then write the answer in the space provided.

1. Type question 1

2. Type question 2

3. Type question 3

4. Type question 4

5. Type question 5

6. Type question 6

7. Type question 7

8. Type question 8

For more information online, go to:

www.microsoftoffice.com

MIXED-DESIGN TEST

2

Easy

Project Number: WD-04

Additional hardware: None

Internet connection required? No

Template available? Yes

Grade Level: Elementary, Middle School, High School

Created by:
Teacher

Project type:
Administrative

Student learning style:
Visual

Approximate time: 30 minutes to create a three-section test

Content Area:
Language Arts
Math

Science

Social Studies

Comments: The mixed-design test has sections for true/false, multiple-choice, and essay test questions. While a simple true/false test may seem like a quick and easy way to administer an exam, these tests tend to have lower validity than some of the other methods. Multiple-choice exams, while they may have somewhat higher test validity and are easy to administer and grade, still only measure a student's ability to recognize the correct answer from a list and do not often require original thought. And while fill-in-the-blank or the written essay response may better measure the level of student knowledge, they are somewhat more complicated to grade. Accordingly, many teachers opt for a mixed-design test, incorporating elements of all three testing methods.

This test can be administered either manually or electronically on the computer. The template on the companion CD includes spaces for teachers to type in the questions and additional spaces for students to record their answers, either by checking a box or by typing in their responses.

Procedures: You may insert your information on the template provided on the companion CD, or you may choose to follow the procedures below.

1. Open a new Microsoft Word document. Designate spaces for "Name, Date, and Subject" at the top of the page.

2. Select **View > Toolbars > Forms.**

3. List the heading "True/False," followed by the directions for the true/false section of the exam and the point value for each question in this section.

4. Enter the question number followed by two **Check Box Form Fields** from the **Forms** toolbar. Follow each box with a "T" and "F," respectively. Move three spaces to the right and add the statement to be evaluated. Repeat step once for each question. On the sample test, we have included five "True/False" questions worth 1 point each.

5. List the heading, "Multiple-Choice," followed by the directions and question point value for this section. For this example we have included nine questions worth 5 points each.

6. List the question number, followed by the question.

7. On the next three or four lines, list the answer and distracters. In front of each possible response, insert a **Check Box Form Field** from the **Form** toolbar. Repeat this step for each desired question.

8. List the heading "Essay Questions," followed by the directions for this section of the test and how many points each question is worth. For the sample test, we have added five essay questions worth 10 points each.

9. Enter each of the essay questions, followed by a space to write the answer. After each question, add a **Text Form Field** from the **Form** toolbar, if you plan for the test to be taken on a computer.

10. The completed exam should look something like this:

Type the name of your test here

Instructor: Type your name here _____

Name: _____
Class: _____
Period: _____
Date: _____

Type test directions here. For example, instruct the student to read each question carefully, then write the answer in the space provided.

True-False: Check "T" or "F" for each question (1 point each)

1. ☐ T   ☐ F   Enter statement 1 here

2. ☐ T   ☐ F   Enter statement 2 here

3. ☐ T   ☐ F   Enter statement 3 here

4. ☐ T   ☐ F   Enter statement 4 here

5. ☐ T   ☐ F   Enter statement 5 here

Multiple Choice. Check the best answer to the question. (5 points each)

6. _____ Type question 6 stem here
   a. ☐ First answer
   b. ☐ Second answer
   c. ☐ Third answer

7. _____ Type question 7 stem here
    a. ☐ First answer
    b. ☐ Second answer
    c. ☐ Third answer

8. _____ Type question 8 stem here
    a. ☐ First answer
    b. ☐ Second answer
    c. ☐ Third answer

9. _____ Type question 9 stem here
    a. ☐ First answer
    b. ☐ Second answer
    c. ☐ Third answer

10. _____ Type question 10 stem here
    a. ☐ First answer
    b. ☐ Second answer
    c. ☐ Third answer

11. _____ Type question 11 stem here
    a. ☐ First answer
    b. ☐ Second answer
    c. ☐ Third answer

12. _____ Type question 12 stem here
    a. ☐ First answer
    b. ☐ Second answer
    c. ☐ Third answer

13. _____ Type question 13 stem here
    a. ☐ First answer
    b. ☐ Second answer
    c. ☐ Third answer

14. _____ Type question 14 stem here
    a. ☐ First answer
    b. ☐ Second answer
    c. ☐ Third answer

Essay Questions: Write the answer to each question in the space provided (10 points each)

15. Type question 15 here

16. Type question 16 here

17. Type question 17 here

18. Type question 18 here

19. Type question 19 here

11. To save your document as a template, select **File > Save As**. This will open up a new window. At the bottom of this new window, in the space marked **Save as type**, select **Document Template (*.dot).** This will automatically default to a special templates folder. If you want to store your document elsewhere, navigate to that folder, name your template, then select **Save**. Remember, to save it as a template, you must make sure your document has a ".dot" extension, instead of the standard default value ".doc" (see Project WD-09, Creating Templates, on the companion CD).

For more information go to Microsoft Word Help and search for *templates.*

Scavenger Hunt

Project Number:	WD-05
Additional hardware:	None
Internet connection required?	Yes
Sample available?	Yes
Grade Level:	Elementary, Middle School, High School

(star graphic: **2 Easy**)

Created by:
Student and/or Teacher

Project type:
Instructional

Student learning style: Visual Aural

Approximate time: 15 minutes to create a 10-question hunt

Content Area: Language Arts Math Science Social Studies

Comments: Students of all ages enjoy an occasional break from traditional direct instruction. In this updated version of the party game "scavenger hunt," rather than go and bother the neighbors in their search for items on a list, students are directed to various sites on the Internet as they seek to answer questions and discover information relevant to the topic at hand. This project can be either teacher or student created and may be an effective addition to your library of instructional or assessment tools.

Procedures:

1. Ensure your computer is online, and connected to the Internet.

2. Open a new Microsoft Word document.

3. Type in the questions you want the students to answer using the Internet as a resource.

4. Without closing the Word document (just minimize it), open the Web page that has the information you want your students to locate. Minimize this Web page.

5. Return to your Word document. Identify a key word or series of key words in the question you've just written. Click and drag your mouse over these words to highlight them.

6. Right click your mouse on these words and select **Hyperlink** You should get a screen that looks similar to this:

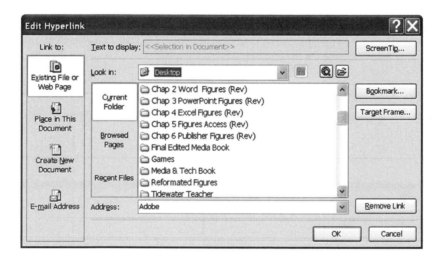

7. Select **Link to Existing File or Web Page**.

8. Reopen the Web page you minimized in Step 4. Click anywhere on the page. This should "capture" the Web page address and automatically place it in the "Address" box on the "Insert Hyperlink" window. If this does not transfer the address automatically, you need to either "cut-and-paste" or manually enter the Web address into the space provided.

9. Select **OK** to return to the Word document. The word(s) you have hyperlinked should now be blue and underlined.

10. Test the link by moving the cursor over the hyperlinked word(s). One of two things will happen, depending on your version of software: (a) The cursor turns into a gloved hand, one finger pointing up, and you can simply click the mouse to activate the link, or (b) the words "CTRL + click to follow link" will appear. If so, hold down the **Control** button while clicking the mouse. Either way, the action should open up the desired Web page.

11. Continue in this manner until you have the desired number of questions in your completed scavenger hunt.

Internet Scavenger Hunt 9th Grade Geometry

1. What is the order of <u>operations</u> and the acronym?
2. What are the three types of <u>triangles,</u> (categorized by their sides)?
3. Is every rectangle a square or is <u>every square</u> a rectangle?
4. How many degrees are in a <u>line</u> and in a <u>circle</u>?
5. How many lines of <u>symmetry</u> are there in a circle?

For more information online, go to:

http://www.education-world.com/a_curr/curr113.shtml

This sample Internet scavenger hunt was created by Niki Zacharopoulos.

GRADE-LEVEL READABILITY TEST

2

Easy

Project Number: WD-06

Additional hardware: None

Internet connection required? No

Template available? No

Grade Level: Elementary, Middle School, High School

Created by:

Teacher

Project type:

Administrative

Student learning style:

Visual

Approximate time: 5 minutes to create a reading grade-level test

Content Area:

Language Arts

Math

Science

Social Studies

Comments: Have you ever assigned a portion of text for your students to read only to learn that what you thought should have been, for example, written for students with third-grade reading skills, was actually written at the fifth-grade level? Or perhaps you've wondered what really constitute independent, instructional, or frustrational reading levels for your students. Microsoft Word has a great little feature that allows you to do a Flesch-Kincaid Test for grade-level reading. This test can be used to determine the reading level of a text you are using or to determine the level of vocabulary used in student writing samples.

   Note: The Flesch-Kincaid grade-level statistic is only one of several reading formulas available on the market today. As with other measures, formula scores are better thought of as rough guides than as highly accurate values.

Word

Procedures:

1. Open a new Microsoft Word document.

2. From the drop-down menu at the top of the page, select **Tools > Options**.

3. Select the tab marked **Spelling and Grammar**. Check the box marked **Show Readability Statistics.** NOTE: The **Check Grammar With Spelling** box must be checked for the **Show Readability Statistics** box to be active.

4. Randomly select a passage of text from the book in question of 50 to 100 words in length. Type this passage into the Microsoft Word document. (Note: The larger the passage, the more accurate the assessment).

5. Highlight/select the passage to be evaluated by clicking and dragging the cursor over the written text.

6. On the drop-down menu at the top of the page, select **Tools > Spelling and Grammar.** Select **OK** to close the Window.

7. The window that opens will have some statistics on the passage just checked. The last of these figures will be a Flesch-Kincaid Grade Level.

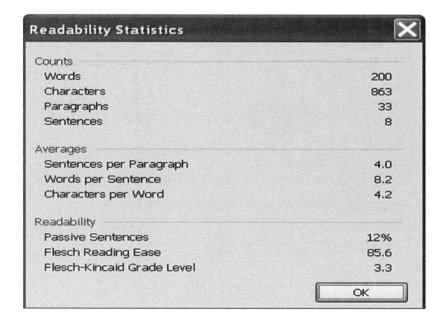

Readability Statistics

Counts	
Words	200
Characters	863
Paragraphs	33
Sentences	8

Averages	
Sentences per Paragraph	4.0
Words per Sentence	8.2
Characters per Word	4.2

Readability	
Passive Sentences	12%
Flesch Reading Ease	85.6
Flesch-Kincaid Grade Level	3.3

OK

8. Use this number as another tool in determining the grade-level appropriateness of reading assignments.

9. To determine the vocabulary grade level of a student's written work, simply type in a 50- to 100-word writing sample and test as described above.

For more information go to Microsoft Word Help and search for *readability.*

NOTES

CHARTS AND GRAPHS

2
Easy

Project Number:	WD-07
Additional hardware:	None
Internet connection required?	No
Template available?	No
Grade Level:	Elementary, Middle School, High School

Created by:

Student and/or
Teacher

Project type:

Instructional

Student and learning style:

Visual

Approximate time: 15 minutes to create a simple data chart

Content Area:

Math

Science

Social Studies

Comments: Math and science students are often faced with the challenge of presenting complicated data in a clear, easily understood format. The ability to chart and graph data is a requirement in most state math and science standardized curriculum. Microsoft Office graphing functions are perfect for this kind of work.

Procedures:

1. For this specific example, let us say the social studies teacher wants to explain how the students voted in the recent student council elections. The final vote tally for class president is as follows:
   - Skippy Tomylou - 135 votes
   - Betty Brickle - 278 votes
   - Biff Bufferson - 198 votes
   - Tessie Tomcat - 25 votes
   - Alice Alsoran - 17 votes

2. Open a Microsoft Word Document.

3. Select **Insert > Picture > Chart** from the drop-down menu at the top of the page.

4. On the datasheet that appears near the sample chart, enter the names of the candidates in the top row.

5. Change the row name to "Votes" and enter the coresponding number of votes each candidate received in Row 1, under the student names.

6. For this example, delete all information in the sample chart Rows 2 and 3. You should end up with a table that looks like the following:

Document2 - Datasheet		A	B	C	D	E	
		Skippy	Betty	Biff	Tessie	Alice	
1	Votes	135	278	198	25	17	
2							
3							

7. The corresponding bar chart for these data will look like this:

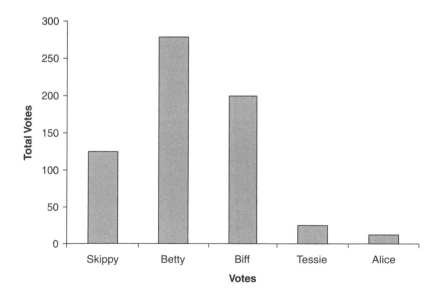

8. Select the chart by clicking on it. Select **Chart > Chart Options** from the drop-down menu to change the appearance of your chart.

9. You can change the basic design of the presentation by selecting **Chart > Chart Type** from the drop-down menu. For example, the same data presented as a **Pie-Chart** might look like this:

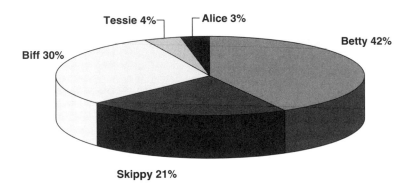

10. By experimenting with different **Chart Types** and **Chart Options**, you can create any number of different visual displays of the data.

For more information go to Microsoft Word Help and search for *chart*.

DAILY JOURNAL

Project Number:	WD-08
Additional hardware:	None
Internet connection required?	No
Template available?	Yes
Grade Level:	Elementary, Middle School, High School

 2 Easy

Created by:

Student

Project type:

Instructional

Student learning style:

Visual

Approximate time: 15 minutes to create a journal template

Content Area:

Language Arts

Math

Science

Social Studies

Comments: Current brain research notes the importance of reflective journaling as a tool to promote higher-order thinking skills. There is a significant increase in student retention if, following a lesson, students are asked to write about the lesson in a journal.

Students should be encouraged to keep a separate journal for each topic, with opportunity given to make entries at the end of each class session. In this project, you will develop a journal template, with designated spaces for students to offer specific reflections on the day's lesson. A template for a journal page is included on the companion CD.

Procedures: You may insert your information on the template provided on the companion CD, or you may choose to follow the procedures below.

1. Open a new document in Microsoft Word.

2. On the toolbar, select **View > Toolbars > Forms**. This will show a toolbar like this:

3. Click on **Insert Frame**. Drag a box where you will want the student to enter information, and type the description of the desired information inside the box. Following the description, add a **Text Form Field** from the **Forms** toolbar. This will place a gray space next to your text. The completed writing box will look something like this:

> What did I learn today? ▨

4. Add a total of three writing text boxes, each containing one of the following statements:

   - What did I learn today?
   - How does this relate to something I learned earlier?
   - How can I use this in the future?

In each case, follow up with a **Text Form Field** to allow student writing.

5. After you have completed your entries, click the **Protect Form** (padlock icon). This will prevent those who use the form from making changes to the design.

6. Now, to save your document as a template. Select **File > Save As**. This will open up a new window. At the bottom of this new window, in the space marked **Save as type**, select **Document Template (*.dot).** This will automatically default to a special templates folder. If you want to store your document elsewhere, navigate to that folder, name your template, then select **Save**. To save it as a template, you must make sure your document has a ".dot" extension, instead of the standard default value ".doc" (see Project WD-09, Creating Templates, on the companion CD).

7. As students access this template, enter their observations, and save their work, it will automatically be saved as a Word document. The original template remains unchanged, even after many users.

Name: ▨

Date: ▨

Class: ▨

Reflective Journal

What did I learn today? ▨

How does this relate to something I learned earlier? ▨

How can I use this in the future? ▨

For more information online, go to:

http://www.sdcoe.k12.ca.us/score/actbank/sjournal.htm

CREATING TEMPLATES

3

Medium Difficulty

Project Number: WD-09

Additional hardware: None

Internet connection required? No

Template available? No

Grade Level: Elementary, Middle School, High School

Created by:

Teacher

Project type:

Instructional

Administrative

Student learning style:

Visual

Approximate time: 30 minutes to create a one-page template

Content Area:

Language Arts

Math

Science

Social Studies

Comments: Fill-in-the-blank documents you create can be used repeatedly if you first save them as templates. Many documents—permission slips, multiple-choice tests, letters to parents, student worksheets, and so on—can be created and saved quickly and easily as a template. When a student uses a template and saves his or her completed work, the new work is automatically saved as a Word document. The basic template remains intact, available for use by the next student.

Procedures:

1. Open a new Microsoft Word document.

2. Design your document. Place a series of five asterisks to mark where you want to have a fill-in blank.

3. After you have completed the layout of your document, open the **Forms** toolbar by selecting **View > Toolbars > Forms.**

4. Left click and drag the mouse over one of the asterisk sections in the completed document. With the asterisks still highlighted, select **Text Form Field** from the **Forms** toolbar. Repeat for all the asterisk designated sections.

5. After all changes have been made, select **Protect Form** (the padlock icon) from the **Forms** toolbar. This will lock your document so that the only changes that can be made are in the spaces you designated with the **Text Form Field**.

6. Now, to save your document as a template. Select **File > Save As**. This will open up a new window. At the bottom of this new window, in the space marked **Save as type**, select **Document Template (*.dot).** This will automatically default to a special templates folder. If you want to store your document elsewhere, navigate to that folder, name your template, then select **Save**. To save it as a template, you must make sure your document has a ".dot" extension, instead of the standard default value ".doc."

7. Microsoft templates are designed so that when you open one, fill in the information, then resave the completed form, it will save as a Word Document (.doc) rather than a Word Template (.dot). This way, each student who opens the template gets a clean document.

8. Microsoft Word contains a large number of premade templates, available for you to modify and use as you like.

For more information, go to Microsoft Word Help and search for *templates.*

MATH TEMPLATES

Project Number:	WD-10
Additional hardware:	None
Internet connection required?	No
Template available?	Yes
Grade Level:	Elementary, Middle School, High School

 3 Medium Difficulty

Created by:
Teacher

Project type:
Instructional

Administrative

Student learning style:
Visual

Approximate time: 30 minutes to create a 15-problem template

Content Area:
Math

Comments: Math operations are often learned through repetition. Microsoft Word templates can help in reviewing and reinforcing mathematical principles taught in class. Properly designed, math templates can help in reinforcing students as they practice the algorithms and help in specific error analysis when they make mistakes. These particular templates can help a student solve math problems by providing partial answers, much like a crossword puzzle with some of the letters missing.

For a sample template, see the companion CD. These templates might prove particularly helpful for students with special learning needs.

Procedures: You may insert your information on the template provided on the companion CD, or you may choose to follow the procedures below.

1. Open a new Microsoft Word document.

2. Open the **Forms** toolbar by selecting **View > Toolbars > Forms.**

3. Type in the equations you want the student to solve, along with the correct answers. Keep your digits aligned vertically.

4. Replace some of the digits in the answer with a **Text Form Field** from the **Form** menu.

5. Select **Form Field Options**. Set **Maximum Length** to "1."

6. By selecting various digits in the answer and replacing them with text form fields, you will be providing the student with only part of the answer. It will be up to the student to complete the solution.

7. Select **Protect Form** from the **Form Menu.**

8. Now, to save your document as a template. Select **File > Save As**. This will open up a new window. At the bottom of this new window, in the space marked **Save as type**, select **Document Template (*.dot).** This will automatically default to a special templates folder. If you want to store your document elsewhere, navigate to that folder, name your template, then **Save**. To save it as a template, you must make sure your document has a ".dot" extension, instead of the standard default value ".doc" (see Project WD-09, Creating Templates, on the companion CD).

9. Your finished template may look something like this:

Name: ▒▒▒▒

Date: ▒▒▒▒

Arithmetic Operations

1. Complete the following problems:

a)	2 4 5	b)	6 7 4	c)	1 3 7	d)	8 2 1
	+1 9 8		+2 6 5		+2 2 2		+3 3 3
	4 ▒ 3		▒ 3 9		▒ 5 ▒		1 ▒ ▒ 4

e)	3 4 5	f)	5 8 2	g)	8 2 1	h)	2 2 1
	− 1 1 2		− 3 4 2		− 7 5 1		− 2 0 9
	2 ▒ 3		▒ 4 0		7 ▒		▒ 2

i)	1 2 8	j)	3 0 2	k)	4 5	l)	7 0 4
	× 4		× 2 0		× 1 2		× 2 2
	▒ 1 2		0 ▒ 0		▒ 0		1 ▒ 0 8
			▒ 0 4		▒ 5		1 ▒ 0 ▒
			6 ▒ 4		5 ▒ ▒		▒ 5 ▒ 8 ▒

CLASS NEWSLETTER

3

Medium Difficulty

Project Number:	WD-11
Additional hardware:	Scanner
Internet connection required?	No
Template available?	No
Grade Level:	Elementary, Middle School, High School

Created by:
Student and/or Teacher

Project type:
Administrative

Student learning style:
Visual

Approximate time: 60 minutes to create a newsletter

Content Area:
Language Arts

Science

Social Studies

Comments: Communication with parents is crucial to your success as a teacher. The class newsletter provides an interesting and attractive way to keep parents informed and to elicit their support for classroom activities. A partial list of the many things that can be addressed in a class newsletter include the following:

- ○ Teacher note of introduction
- ○ Schedule of activities

o Homework plan
o Class rules
o Discipline plan
o Missed-class procedures
o Holiday parties
o Field trip information
o Field trip permission slips
o Chaperone requests
o Class parent/volunteer coordinator
o PTA information
o Supplies list
o Token economy system (if used)
o School and teacher contact info
o Upcoming events (science fair, band concert, etc.)

As you can see, the problem will not be in deciding how to get enough material to warrant a newsletter. The problem will be in deciding what NOT to include.

While the instructions here are how to develop a class newsletter using Microsoft Word, you may find Microsoft Publisher, if you have it, a more versatile program for projects of this nature.

Procedures:

1. Open a new Microsoft Word document.

2. For landscape orientation, select **File > Page Setup**. Click the **Margins** tab and select **Landscape**. If you prefer a more vertical arrangement, remain in **Portrait** mode.

3. Go to **Format > Borders and Shading** and select your desired border design and thickness.

4. Decide on the number of columns you want. Select **Format > Columns**, then pick from the available selections. Using a two- or three-column design will help brighten up your newsletter.

5. If you want to add clipart or pictures, first draw a text box of the desired dimensions near the center of your page. Select **Insert > Picture** and select your source. Place the picture inside the text box. You should then be able to move the picture to a place of your choosing.

6. Right click on the picture. Select **Format Picture > Layout.**

7. Choose your desired **Wrapping Style** from the available options. This last step will allow you to place images anywhere on the page, and the words will wrap around the image.

8. By selecting different **Fonts** and **WordArt**, you can create some interesting and informative newsletters to send home with your students.

For more information online, go to:

http://www.g4tv.com/callforhelparchive/features/34710/Make_a_Newsletter.html

CLOZE TEST

Project Number:	WD-12	**3** **Medium Difficulty**

Additional hardware: None

Internet connection required? No

Template available? Yes

Grade Level: Elementary, Middle School, High School

Created by: **Teacher**

Project type: **Administrative**

Student learning style: **Visual**

Approximate time: 20 minutes to create one test

Content Area: **Language Arts** **Science** **Social Studies**

Comments: A cloze test is another useful tool for determining the student's entry level of knowledge about a given topic. This may be used to determine what students already know about a subject when introducing a new topic, or it is also commonly used to determine whether a student will be able to read the text at the independent, instructional, or frustrational reading level.

Procedures: You may insert your information on the template provided on the companion CD, or you may choose to follow the procedures below.

1. Open a new Microsoft Word document.

2. Type in a passage of at least 250 words in length.

3. Replace every fifth word with a sequentially numbered blank space. Ensure that the blank spaces are the same length, (normally 6-8 spaces). The following example is a cloze test on the Gettysburg Address:

Name: ▒▒▒   Date: ▒▒▒

Gettysburg Address – Cloze Test

Four score and seven (1) ▒▒▒ ago our fathers brought (2) ▒▒▒, upon this continent, a ▒▒▒ (3) ▒▒▒ nation, conceived in Liberty, (4) ▒▒▒ dedicated to the proposition (5) ▒▒▒ all men are created (6) ▒▒▒

Now we are engaged (7) ▒▒▒ a great civil war, (8) ▒▒▒ whether that nation, or (9) ▒▒▒ nation, so conceived, and (10) ▒▒▒ dedicated, can long endure. (11) ▒▒▒ are met here on (12) ▒▒▒ great battlefield of that (13) ▒▒▒. We have come to (14) ▒▒▒ a portion of it ▒▒▒ (15) ▒▒▒ a final resting place (16) ▒▒▒ those who here gave (17) ▒▒▒ lives that that nation (18) ▒▒▒ live. It is altogether (19) ▒▒▒ and proper that we (20) ▒▒▒ do this.

But in (21) ▒▒▒ larger sense we can (22) ▒▒▒ dedicate — we can not (23) ▒▒▒ — we can not hallow (24) ▒▒▒ ground. The brave men, (25) ▒▒▒ and dead, who struggled, (26) ▒▒▒, have consecrated it far (27) ▒▒▒ our poor power to (28) ▒▒▒ or detract. The world (29) ▒▒▒ little note, nor long (30) ▒▒▒, what we say here, (31) ▒▒▒ can never forget what (32) ▒▒▒ did here. It is (33) ▒▒▒ us, the living, rather (34) ▒▒▒ be dedicated here to (35) ▒▒▒ unfinished work which they (36) ▒▒▒, thus far, so nobly (37) ▒▒▒ on. It is rather (38) ▒▒▒ us to be here (39) ▒▒▒ to the great task (40) ▒▒▒ before us — that from (40) ▒▒▒ honored dead we take (41) ▒▒▒ devotion to that cause (42) ▒▒▒ which they here gave (43) ▒▒▒ last full measure of (44) ▒▒▒ — that we here highly (45) ▒▒▒ that these dead shall (46) ▒▒▒ have died in vain; (47) ▒▒▒ this nation shall have (48) ▒▒▒ new birth of freedom; (49) ▒▒▒ that this government of (50) ▒▒▒ people, by the people, for the people, shall not perish from the earth.

---

4. Administer the cloze test to the students. It is important that the student's answer match the deleted word exactly. Resist the temptation to give credit for an answer that means the same thing as the correct answer, if the cloze test is to yield reliable information. To score the cloze, count all the words that are semantically and syntactically correct. Do not count spelling.

   Score as follows

60% and above	Material is too easy	Independent level
40%–60%	Material is about right	Instructional level
Under 40%	Material is too difficult	Frustration level

5. This cloze test can be made into a template for repeat administrations in electronic format. See WD-09 Cloze Gettysburg Address template on the companion CD as an example.

For more information online, go to:

http://eall.hawaii.edu/yao/la2004/Cloze.htm

MAZE TEST

3

Medium Difficulty

Project Number: WD-13

Additional hardware: None

Internet connection required? No

Template available? Yes

Grade Level: Elementary, Middle School, High School

Created by:

Teacher

Project type:

Administrative

Student learning style:

Visual

Approximate time: 30 minutes to create a 200-word maze

Content Area:

Language Arts

Science

Social Studies

Comments: The maze is a modification of the cloze procedure described in Project WD-09. Students read silently while taking this multiple-choice test. This can also be used to evaluate prior knowledge about a subject or to determine the readability of a certain passage. In the maze, the student chooses the correct word from three possible choices. This may be used for students with special learning needs while the rest of the class takes a cloze test (Project WD-09) on the same passage.

Procedures: You may insert your information on the template provided on the companion CD, or you may choose to follow the procedures below.

1. Open a Microsoft Word document.

2. Type in a passage of text, between 150 and 400 words in length. The example shown is from Aesop's fable, "The Bear and Two Travelers."

   Two men were traveling together, when a Bear suddenly met them on their path. One of them raced ahead of his companion and climbed up quickly into a tree and concealed himself in the branches. The other, seeing that he must be attacked, fell flat on the ground, and when the Bear came up and felt him with his snout, and smelt him all over, he held his breath, and feigned the appearance of death as much as he could. The Bear soon left him, for it is said he will not touch a dead body. When he was quite gone, the other traveler descended from the tree, and jocularly inquired of his friend what it was the Bear had whispered in his ear. "He gave me this advice," his companion replied. "Never travel with a friend who deserts you at the approach of danger." Misfortune tests the sincerity of friends.

3. Select every seventh word in the document. Replace this word with three choices. One of these is the exact word in the original text, and the other two are distracters. Select one distracter that is similar to the original word and might possibly fit in the sentence. Select the third word from somewhere else. The student must circle or check the correct word, depending on format.

   Two men were traveling together, when a Bear suddenly (ATE, MET, SAT) them on their path. One of (THE, THEM, AT) raced ahead of his companion and (STARTED, DREW, CLIMBED) up quickly into a tree and (TIED, CONCEALED, SLAPPED) himself in the branches. The other, (WONDERED, SNOUT, SEEING) that he must be attacked, fell (OVER, FLAT, FLOOD) on the ground, and when the (BEAR, BOAR, BOARD) came up and felt him with (OUT, IT, HIS) snout, and smelt him all over, (SHE, HE, WHY) held his breath, and feigned the (SMELL, TASTE, APPEARANCE) of death as much as he (COULD, LIKED, ATE). The Bear soon left him, for (ALL, IT, HAD) is said he will not touch (YOUR, SOME, A) dead body. When he was quite (QUIET, GONE, RIGHT), the other Traveler descended from the (HOUSE, RACE, TREE), and jocularly inquired of his friend (WHAT, WHY, ALSO) it was the Bear had whispered (OVER, IN, TOWARDS) his ear. "He gave me this (ADVICE, KEY, TAPE)," his companion replied. "Never travel with (TWO, NO, A) friend who deserts you at the (APPROACH, SOUND, SPEED) of danger." Misfortune tests the sincerity of friends.

4. The maze is graded in similar fashion to the cloze test:

60% and above	Material is too easy	Independent level
40%–60%	Material is about right	Instructional level
Under 40%	Material is too difficult	Frustration level

5. If this is a maze you expect to give to many students, perhaps on a computer, you may wish to make a template of the document. The WD-10 Maze Aesop Fable template on the companion CD has a sample maze with boxes to check to indicate the answers selected.

PEER EDITING AND REVIEWER COMMENTS

3
Medium
Difficulty

Project Number:	WD-14
Additional hardware:	None
Internet connection required?	No
Template available?	No
Grade Level:	Elementary, Middle School, High School

Created by:
Student and/or
Teacher

Project type:
Instructional

Student learning style:
Visual

Approximate time: 10 minutes to create comments for a two-page writing assignment

Content Area:
Language Arts

Science

Social Studies

Comments: "Editing" is one of the key steps to the writing process. Often, this is done by simply having the students exchange papers, examine them for errors and suggested improvements, and return it to the original author for correction and submission. While this may prove simple in cases where assignments are peer edited during class, it becomes more challenging if students are not in the same vicinity at the time of submission, or if the document was generated on a word processing computer. Not to worry. Microsoft Word has features that allow editing and commenting on documents submitted electronically. Students can now write a paper using Microsoft Word, make it an attachment to an e-mail, and send it to a peer editor. The peer editor can then open the document, add editorial comments, and send it back to the author. These comments can be read and accepted or rejected by the original author, then incorporated in the document. Pretty slick!

Teachers can use these same features when grading student papers.

Procedures:

1. Open the document to be reviewed. On the drop-down menu, select **Tools > Options**.

2. Select the tab marked **Track Changes**. Review the various menu selections available on this page and select your preferred way to indicate insertions and deletions. Press **OK** to return to the document.

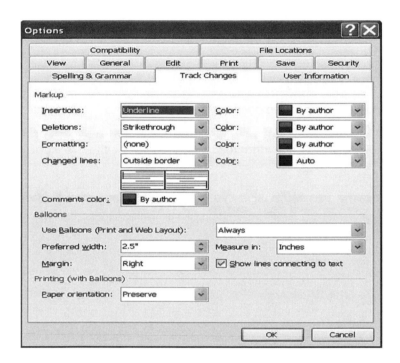

3. From the drop-down menu, select **View > Toolbars > Reviewing**. This will open the **Reviewing** toolbar.

4. As you review the text in the document being edited and come to a point where you want to add a comment, select **Insert Comment** from the Reviewing Toolbar. Any changes, additions, or deletions you make to the document will be noted alongside the original text.

In the following example, we have chosen to review the Preamble to the Constitution.

We, the People, of the United States, in order to form a more perfect Union, establish justice, ensure domestic tranquility, provide for the common defense, promote the general welfare, and secure the blessings of liberty to ourselves and our posterity, do ordain and establish this constitution for the United States of America.

5. After making edits to the document above, the document may look like this:

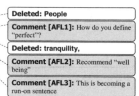

We, the majority of the people, of the United States of America, in order to form a more perfect Union, establish justice, ensure domestic peace provide for the common defense, promote the general welfare, and secure the blessings of liberty to ourselves and our posterity, do ordain and establish this Constitution for the United States of America on the North American continent.

Deleted: People

Comment [AFL1]: How do you define "perfect"?

Deleted: tranquility,

Comment [AFL2]: Recommend "well being"

Comment [AFL3]: This is becoming a run-on sentence

6. This edited document can then be electronically transmitted back to the original author.

7. Upon receipt of the edited document, determine whether to accept or reject the suggested edits by going to the **Reviewing** toolbar and select either **Accept Change** or **Reject Change**.

For more information, go to Microsoft Word Help and search for *reviewing text.*

NOTES

DECISION-MAKING AID

Project Number:	WD-15
Additional hardware:	None
Internet connection required?	No
Template available?	Yes
Grade Level:	Elementary, Middle School, High School

Medium Difficulty

Created by:
Teacher

Project type:
Instructional

Student learning style:
Visual

Approximate time: 30 minutes to create a five-option decision aid

Content Area:
Language Arts

Science

Social Studies

Comments: One of the more important tasks in teaching is to help our students develop higher-order, critical thinking skills. When faced with a complex problem, students may be faced with several options, any one of which may seem to be an acceptable solution. This decision-making aid is based on the work of Richard Bolles, who wrote *What Color Is Your Parachute?* It can help a student prioritize the available options from "most preferred" to "least preferred." The Decision-Making Aid included on the resource companion CD can help you prioritize among several possible solutions to a problem.

Procedures: You may insert your information on the template provided on the companion CD, or you may choose to follow the procedures below.

1. Open a new Microsoft Word document.
2. Select **View > Toolbars > Forms**.
3. Using the **Insert Frame** button, draw several frames on the page in the pattern seen on the Decision Aid Template and in the example figure below.

The question is:

Option One

1 ☐ 2 ☐	Option Two

1 ☐ 3 ☐	2 ☐ 3 ☐	Option Three

1 ☐ 4 ☐	2 ☐ 4 ☐	3 ☐ 4 ☐	Option Four

1 ☐ 5 ☐	2 ☐ 5 ☐	3 ☐ 5 ☐	4 ☐ 5 ☐	Option Five

1	2	3	4	5	OPTION NUMBER
					How many total times option was selected
					Final Ranking of This Option (From 1 to 5)

Step #1	Identify the basic question you are trying to decide, and enter in the space provided
Step #2	Identify up to five options and enter these in the spaces provided.
Step #3	Compare each of the options two at a time. Check the box for your preferred option.
Step #4	Count up the TOTAL number of times each option was selected and enter in the space below the OPTION NUMBER.
Step #5	Identify the final ranking of the options based on number of times each was selected. In the event of a tie, look at the comparison of those two options (Step #3). Give a higher preference to the winner in that comparison.

4. Using the **Text Form Field** and the **Check Box Form Field**, place these as needed throughout the document. Insert text in the designated boxes as shown in the example.

5. Once you finish creating the form, select **Protect Form** from the **Forms** toolbar. Save as a template so that the basic document can be reused and remain intact.

6. Use the completed form as follows:

   a. Identify the basic question you are trying to decide, and enter it in the space provided.
   b. Identify up to five options, and enter these in the spaces provided.
   c. Compare each of the options two at a time. Check the box with the number of your preferred choice between the two.
   d. Count up the TOTAL number of times each option was selected and enter in the space below the OPTION NUMBER.
   e. Identify the final ranking of the options based on number of times each was selected. In the event of a tie, look at the comparison of the two tied options (Step #3). Give a higher preference to the winner in that comparison.

7. Now, look to see if you are pleased with the resulting ranking of your choices. If you are not pleased with the choice that ranked Number 1 and would have preferred another answer, choose that option instead. After all, this is meant only to be a decision aid. You still are the one who must make the decision and live with the results.

For more information online, go to:

http://www.southampton.liu.edu/fw/portfolio_resource_guide/g3.htm

NOTES

MEMORIZING TEXT PASSAGES

3
Medium Difficulty

Project Number:	WD-16
Additional hardware:	None
Internet connection required?	No
Sample available?	Yes
Grade Level:	Elementary, Middle School, High School

Created by:

Teacher

Project type:

Instructional

Student learning style:

Visual

Approximate time: 30 minutes to create one memory template

Content Area:

Language Arts

Social Studies

Comments: The Constitution is the fundamental document of our system of government. Nations worldwide have patterned their governing bodies after the design laid down in this document. The Preamble introduces the purpose and aims of this illustrious document, and committing this portion of the Constitution to memory helps students understand the precepts of democracy. The sample found on the companion CD can be used to help students commit these 52 words to memory.

This same technique of selectively removing parts of a document and having students replace them, can be used for any number of tasks that require memorizing text.

Procedures:

1. Open a new Microsoft Word document.

2. Type in the desired text. Copy and paste this text five more times, either on the same page or, preferably, on different pages.

3. Select **View > Toolbars > Forms.**

4. Leave the first rendition intact. On the second and following copies of the text, substitute a few of the key words with **Text Form Field** from the **Forms Toolbar**. Increase the number of words substituted with **Text Form Field** as you move from text passage to text passage. The final passage should require the student to totally rewrite the entire text passage from memory.

5. Your final document may resemble this example. (Note: The paragraphs here are shown on one page for illustration purposes only. You should print each rendition on a separate piece of paper.)

---

1. **Read the preamble to the Constitution of the United States three times.**

We the People, of the United Sates, in order to form a more perfect union, establish justice, ensure domestic tranquility, provide for the common defense, promote the general welfare, and secure the blessings of liberty to ourselves and our posterity, do ordain and establish this constitution for the United States of America.

2. **Now, enter the missing words in the spaces provided.**

We the People, of the United ▇▇▇, in order to form a more perfect ▇▇▇, establish justice, ensure domestic ▇▇▇, provide for the common defense, promote the general ▇▇▇, and secure the blessings of ▇▇▇ to ourselves and our posterity, do ordain and establish this ▇▇▇ for the United States of America.

3. **Once again, enter the missing words in the spaces provided.**

We the ▇▇▇, of the United ▇▇▇, in order to form a more perfect ▇▇▇, establish ▇▇▇, ensure domestic ▇▇▇, provide for the common ▇▇▇, promote the general ▇▇▇, and secure the blessings of ▇▇▇ to ourselves and our ▇▇▇, do and establish this ▇▇▇ for the United States of ▇▇▇.

4. **Now we've really removed a lot of words. Fill them back in.**

We the ▇▇▇, of the ▇▇▇ States, in order to ▇▇▇ a more ▇▇▇ union, establish ▇▇▇, ensure ▇▇▇ tranquility, provide for the ▇▇▇ defense, ▇▇▇ the general ▇▇▇, and secure the ▇▇▇ of ▇▇▇ to ourselves and our ▇▇▇, do ordain and ▇▇▇ this constitution for the ▇▇▇ States of ▇▇▇.

5. **This time we've deleted groups of words. Try and replace them from memory.**

We the ▇▇▇, of the ▇▇▇, in order to form a ▇▇▇, establish ▇▇▇ ensure ▇▇▇, provide for the ▇▇▇, promote the ▇▇▇, and secure the ▇▇▇ to ▇▇▇, do ▇▇▇ this ▇▇▇ for the ▇▇▇.

6. **Made it this far, huh? Show me what you know. Write out the entire Preamble from memory. I've even provided you with the first word to help you out.**

We ▇▇▇

FLASH CARDS

Project Number: WD-17

Additional hardware: Printer

Internet connection required? No

Template available? No

Grade Level: Elementary, Middle School, High School

3
Medium Difficulty

Created by: Student and/or Teacher

Project type: Instructional

Student learning style: Visual   Aural   Kinesthetic

Approximate time: 15 minutes to create a 30-card set

Content Area: Language Arts   Math

Comments: You can help your students recall basic facts more quickly and with greater accuracy using flash cards. Using the label-making features of Microsoft Word, you can quickly create a collection of flash cards to review weekly spelling words, improve recognition of Dolch basic sight words, or even create a fun way to review basic math facts. The teacher can make these cards for review with the entire class. Better yet, why not have the students create their own flash cards for personal use and study.

Procedures:

1. Open a new document in Microsoft Word.

2. Select **Tools > Letters and Mailings > Envelopes and Labels** from the pull-down menu at the top of your screen.

3. Select the **Labels** tab, then **Options**. Here you will be able to choose which manufacturer's label template you wish to use.

4. Select **Avery Standard** from the list of available "Label products."

5. Highlight the product number of the Avery Standard label templates you wish to use. Note that the dimensions of each label are listed when selected. The particular product number you select should be based on the size and shape you want your flash cards to be.

   For math flash cards, I recommend:
   #3259 Note Card—4 per page, 4.5″ × 3.25″

   For spelling word flash cards, consider one of the following:
   #5164 Shipping—6 per page, 3.33″ × 4″
   #5384 Name Badge—6 per page, 3″ × 4″
   #5388 Index Card—3 per page, 3″ × 5″

6. After selecting the desired product number, click **OK**.
   NOTE: Do not enter any information in the Address block at this time.

7. Check the radio button marked **Full page of the same label**.

8. Select **New Document**. You should now have a page displaying several rectangles, wth dimensions of the label selected in Step 5. Note: In some versions of Microsoft Word, the outlines of the rectangles may not be visible. Even so, use the tab key to move from box to box.

9. Enter the first spelling word in the first box. Select **Tab** to move to the second box. Adjust font size and word alignment using selections from the **Formatting** toolbar.

10. After entering all the desired spelling words, select **File > Save <u>A</u>s**, then choose where you want to store the document.

11. To print flash cards, place heavy-duty card stock paper in the paper tray of the default printer and select **File > Print > OK**. Note: If card stock jams during printing, you may need to feed the card stock through the alternate feed slot (usually on the front of the printer) rather than using the normal feed tray.

12. Using scissors or a paper cutter, cut the cards to the desired size and shape.

Caution: Closely monitor the children if they are using a paper cutter.

For more information online, go to:

www.english-zone.com/reading/dolch.html

COURSE SYLLABUS

Project Number:	WD-18
Additional hardware:	None
Internet connection required?	No
Template available?	Yes
Grade Level:	High School

3

Medium Difficulty

Created by:

Teacher

Project type:

Administrative

Student learning style:

Visual

Approximate time: 45 minutes to create one course syllabus

Content Area:

Language Arts

Math

Science

Social Studies

Comments: While a course syllabus is generally found in higher education at the undergraduate or graduate course level, this document may also be useful in high school classes. The syllabus will fully describe the purposes, contact information, goals and objectives, required assignments, and grading criteria for the course.

Some schools may have very specific instructions and require a specific format in designing the syllabus. Otherwise, you may use the syllabus template on the companion CD if you have the latitude at your particular school to do so.

Procedures: You may insert your information on the template provided on the companion CD, or you may choose to follow the procedures below.

1. Open a new document in Microsoft Word.

2. Begin the document with the course identifiying information.

3. Insert your name, phone number, office location, e-mail address, and office hours if any.

4. List the title of any required and optional texts. Be sure to include ISBN numbers for easy identification when ordering books online.

5. Insert a description of the course.

6. List any special projects and required activities.

7. Identify any additional resources available. Be sure to include Web site addresses, if applicable.

8. Describe the grading criteria that will be used in the course.

9. Enter the course schedule, including the dates, topics and required readings, and assignment due dates.

10. Include information on the times and places of exams.

Enter course name—Syllabus

Instructor	Type your name here	E-mail	Type your e-mail address here
Phone	Type phone number here	Office Hours	Type office hours here
Office	Type office location here		

Text:
Type required texts here.

Description:
Type a description of the course here.

Goals:
Type Goal 1 of the course here.
Type Goal 2 of the course here.
Type additional goals here.

Requirements:
Enter required activities and projects here.

Resources:
Enter special facilities, URLs, advisors here.

Evaluation:
Enter critieria for performance evaluation here.

Enter course name

Course Schedule

(Enter week, topic for the week, and required reading in the appropriate columns below. Use the TAB key to move around in the table. To insert rows, click on the table and then on the Table menu, point to Insert and click on the Row action you want to take. To delete rows, click on the table and then on the Table menu, point to Delete and click on Rows.)

Week	Topic	Required Reading

Examinations:
Enter time and place of exams here.

For more information online, go to:

www.microsoftoffice.com

WRITING GUIDE

Project Number:	WD-19
Additional hardware:	None
Internet connection required?	No
Template available?	Yes
Grade Level:	Elementary, Middle School, High School

Medium Difficulty

Created by:

Teacher

Project type:

Instructional

Student learning style:

Visual

Approximate time: 30 minutes to create a three-point guide

Content Area:

Language Arts

Science

Social Studies

Comments: Writing guides aid in the writing process and are very popular tools when teaching students the fundamentals of composition. In this project, you will learn how to create writing guide templates for use in many of your writing assignments. By using a writing guide, your students will be better able to concentrate on what they want to say rather than getting wrapped up in the mechanics of how to say it. The Template WD-19 on the companion CD provides a ready-made example, with room for students to identify key points. This template has designated spaces for the introduction, three main points about the topic, three subpoints for each main point, and a conclusion.

Procedures: You may insert your information on the template provided on the companion CD, or you may choose to follow the procedures below.

1. Open a new document in Microsoft Word.

2. On the toolbar, select **View > Toolbars > Forms.** This will show a toolbar like this:

3. Click on **Insert Frame**. Drag a box where you will want the student to enter information and type the description of the desired information inside the box. Following the description, add a **Text Form Field** from the **Forms** toolbar. This will place a gray space next to your text. The completed writing box will look something like this:

4. Add as many writing text boxes as needed to complete the template as suggested in the figure on the following page. After you have completed your entries, click the **Protect Form** (padlock icon). This will prevent those who use the form from making changes to the design.

5. Now, to save your document as a template. Select **File > Save As**. This will open up a new window. At the bottom of this new window, in the space marked **Save as type**, select **Document Template (*.dot).** This will automatically default to a special templates folder. If you want to store your document elsewhere, navigate to that folder, name your template, then **Save**. To save it as a template, you must make sure your document has a ".dot" extension, instead of the standard default value ".doc" (see Project WD-09, Creating Templates, on the companion CD).

6. This template format will allow students to use the basic design, but when they save their work, it will automatically be saved as a word document. This way the template will remain unchanged for the next student.

For more information online, go to:

http://www.kented.org.uk/ngfl/subjects/literacy/Writing-frames/frames2.html

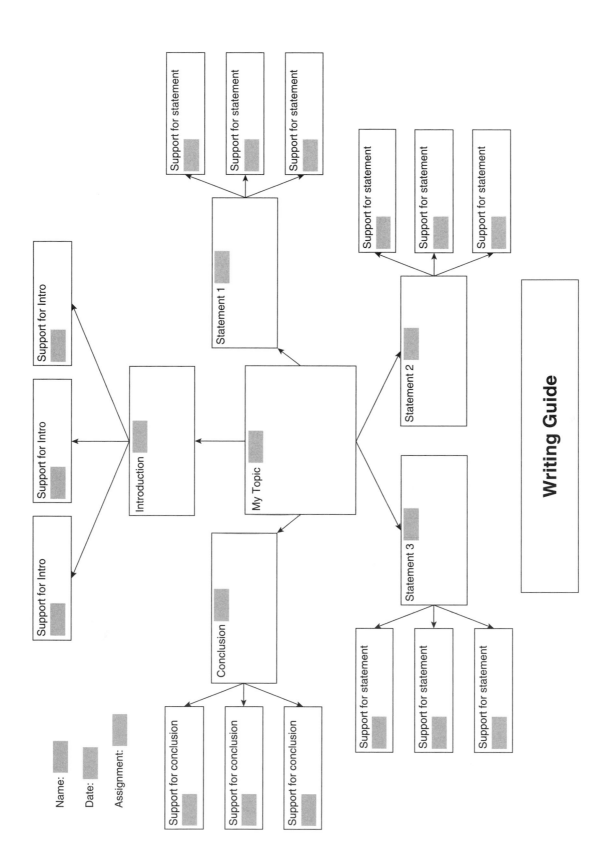

Writing Guide

How to Write Instructions

3

Medium Difficulty

Project Number:	WD-20
Additional hardware:	None
Internet connection required?	No
Template available?	Yes
Grade Level:	Elementary, Middle School, High School

Created by:

Teacher

Project type:

Instructional

Student learning style:

Visual

Approximate time: 15 minutes to create one instruction template

Content Area:

Language Arts   **Math**   **Science**   **Social Studies**

Comments: One way to determine that a process has been well learned is to have the student instruct someone else in the procedure. Whether it is how to use an arithmetic algorithm or how to bake a cake, clear instruction is essential. This project and the accompanying template will help your students walk through the process of writing understandable instructions.

Procedures: You may insert your information on the template provided on the companion CD, or you may choose to follow the procedures below.

1. Open a new Microsoft Word document. Go to **View > Toolbars > Forms.**

2. Using the **Insert Frame** button, create a box in the center of the page, with six other boxes surrounding it in a circle.

3. Inside the center text box, type "1. If you want to know how to . . . " followed by a **Text Form Field** from the forms menu.

4. Repeat the process with the box at the 12 o'clock position. This time, type inside the box "2. You will need these things. . . . " followed by a **Text Form Field**.

5. Repeat the process for each text box, continuing clockwise around the circle. Label inside the text boxes "3. The first thing you do is . . . 4. Next you need to . . . 5. Then you need to . . . 6. After that you . . . 7. Finally, you need to . . ."

6. Insert a **Text Form Field** inside each frame, and add arrows (from the **Drawing** toolbar) to show the progression from step to step.

7. Now save your document as a template. Select **File > Save As**. This will open up a new window. At the bottom of this new window, in the space marked **Save as type**, select **Document Template (*.dot).** This will automatically default to a special templates folder. If you want to store your document elsewhere, navigate to that folder, name your template, then **Save**. To save it as a template, you must make sure your document has a ".dot" extension, instead of the standard default value ".doc" (see Project, WD-09, Creating Templates, on the companion CD). Move to the desired directory and give your document a name.

8. The completed template will look something like this:

How to Write Instructions for Just About Anything

2. You will need these things

3. The first thing you do is

1. If you want to know how to

7. Finally, you need to

4. Next, you need to

6. After that, you

5. Then you need to

For more information go to Microsoft Word Help and search for *templates***.**

3

Microsoft PowerPoint Projects

In this chapter you will find the following activities:

Project Number	Title	Difficulty	Created By
PP-01	Water Cycle	1	Teacher
PP-02	Back-to-School Night	1	Teacher
PP-03	Classroom Seating Chart	1	Teacher
PP-04	Postcards	1	Student and/or Teacher
PP-05	Math Place Value	2	Teacher and/or Student
PP-06	Insects	2	Student and/or Teacher
PP-07	Trading Cards	2	Student
PP-08	Analogies	2	Teacher
PP-09	Weather Report	2	Student
PP-10	Rounding Review	2	Teacher
PP-11	Vocabulary Words Flash Cards	3	Student and/or Teacher
PP-12	Q & A Review	3	Teacher
PP-13	Electronic Portfolio	3	Student
PP-14	Comparing Numbers	3	Teacher
PP-15	Where I Live	3	Student and/or Teacher
PP-16	Multiple-Choice Test	4	Teacher
PP-17	Talking Book	5	Student and/or Teacher
PP-18	WebQuest	5	Student and/or Teacher
PP-19	Pseudo-Jeopardy Quiz Game	5	Student and/or Teacher
PP-20	Critical Reading for Content	5	Teacher

INTRODUCTION TO MICROSOFT POWERPOINT

Without a doubt, Microsoft PowerPoint is one of the most widely used presentation graphics programs in use today. Every day, almost 30 million PowerPoint presentations are made worldwide! The omnipresent PowerPoint is found in classrooms, boardrooms, sales presentations, motivational workshops, and training facilities across the country. With PowerPoint, you can create presentations using colors, animation, audio, and music in ways not possible with a chalkboard or overhead transparencies. Using the built-in wizards, even the most inexperienced PowerPoint user can create professional-looking graphics to support the learning objectives.

Unfortunately, overuse of this technology at the expense of good instructional content and delivery can result in "PowerPoint poisoning." Do not expect the use of technology to make up for poor teaching. Overloading students with irritating, irrelevant, or unnecessary flashiness in a presentation can result in reduced effectiveness of the lesson. Let's face it. A boring, unprepared, or uninspired teacher with dull material will not fare any better with PowerPoint than without it. A quick search of the Internet reveals thousands of articles decrying the misuse of PowerPoint in the classroom—"Ban It Now: Friends Don't Let Friends Use PowerPoint," by Thomas Stewart, or John Raymond's "PowerPointlessness," to name a few.

However, with training and a little thought, you can design instructive and interesting activities, using the power of technology, to help your students succeed in the classroom. PowerPoint presentations can be created by students or teachers to the advantage of both. Design a pseudo-Jeopardy game to assess student learning, or make a "talking book" to improve literacy skills in young children. Use PowerPoint to combine an informative presentation with an Internet scavenger hunt in a project called a WebQuest. Summarize sections of text, illustrate analogies, or evaluate the artistic merits of the old masters using PowerPoint. This book contains 20 different PowerPoint projects you can try, but you will soon see that you are limited only by your imagination and that of your students.

WATER CYCLE

Very Easy

Project Number:	PP-01
Additional hardware:	None
Internet connection required?	No
Template available?	Yes
Grade Level:	Elementary, Middle School

Created by:

Teacher

Project type:

Instructional

Student learning style:

Visual

Aural

Approximate time: 15 minutes to create a water cycle slide

Content Area:

Science

Comments: Your students will need a good understanding of the water cycle before moving into a broader lesson on the weather. This simple, four-step process can be easily explained and demonstrated using PowerPoint, custom animation, and some imagination. Because of the simplicity of this lesson, you may choose to have the students create the PowerPoint shows as part of the unit assessment. An Internet connection, though not essential, will allow you to download sound effects to accompany the various stages. These sound effects will prove helpful to the auditory learner. Likewise, a scanner, while not critical, will allow you to use a variety of images that might not already be available in electronic format.

While this particular example is of the water cycle, you can use this same idea for presenting other cyclical events as well (lunar cycle, rock cycle, seasons, etc.).

Procedures: You may insert your information on the template provided on the companion CD, or you may choose to follow the procedures below.

1. Locate a picture of a lake with land in the background. Ideally, there should be clouds in the sky, but this is not critical, as you can draw these in yourself. Save this picture in an easily located file. To save an image, right click on the image, select **Save Picture As**, and designate where you want to save it.

2. Open Microsoft PowerPoint.

3. On the **Format** menu, select **Slide Layout > Blank Slide**. Name the presentation with the date and subject.

4. Insert the lake picture into the PowerPoint slide. Adjust the size of the image so it fills the entire page.

5. Using **Text Box** from the **Insert** menu, insert the text on the image as desired to indicate the various stages of the water cycle.

6. To add directional arrows, open the drawing toolbar, select **AutoShapes > Block Arrows**, and choose from the available designs.

7. Once you have all the text written in the proper places on the slide and the connecting arrows drawn, you may want to have these become visible one statement at a time using the "animation" feature. Click on the image or text box you want to animate. Then click **Slide Show > Custom Animation** and select the desired special effect option from those available. Experiment with several of these until you find one you like.

8. ADDING PRERECORDED SOUND EFFECTS: If you really want to be creative, add sound to each slide. This can be a sound effect for some words—the sound of a rainstorm in the previous example—or you may want to add your own voice pronouncing the words *precipitation, collection, evaporation,* and *condensation* as needed. To add sound to your project, do the following:

    a. Find the sound you want from the Internet, a sound effects CD, or other source. Make sure it is a .wav sound file, since PowerPoint cannot easily use file types with different extensions like .mp3, among others. Store this sound file in an easily locatable place on your computer.

    b. From the drop-down menu at the top of the screen, select **Insert > Movies and Sounds > Sound from File**. Navigate to the desired file and select **OK**.

    c. Decide whether you want the sound to play automatically when you first open the slide or play only when clicked.

9. ADDING SPOKEN TEXT: You and your students will have fun with this part, as they become junior recording artists. To record spoken words, you will need a pin jack or USB plug microphone. These mics can be found for a reasonable price (usually $20.00 or less) at office supply stores or computer centers.

a. Select the desired slide, being sure you are in the Normal View mode. From the pull-down menu at the top of the screen select **Insert > Movies and Sounds > Record Sounds.**

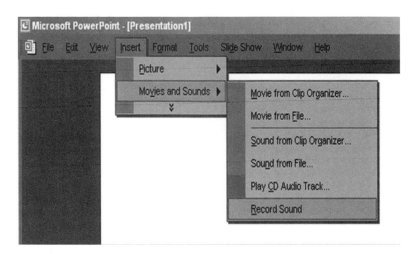

b. The default name listed on the window that appears is **Recorded Sound**. Replace this name with one of your own choosing, but make it unique to that particular slide. Position the **Record Sound** window so it doesn't cover the text you want to read. Press the red-circle record button, wait one second, read the desired text, wait one second, push the blue-rectangle stop button. Pressing the blue-triangle playback button will allow you to review what you have just recorded.

c. If you like what you hear, enter a name for the sound in the space provided and press **OK** to save your recording and move on to the next slide. A small speaker icon will appear in the center of the slide. You can click and drag this icon anywhere you want on the slide. By clicking on this icon while in **View Slide Show** mode, you should hear the recorded audio clip. If you want the sound clip to play automatically, go to the **Slide Sorter View** and select **Slide Transition**. At this point, locate the word **Sound** and click on the pull-down menu. Find and select the desired sound file. This sound should now play automatically when you come to the slide in the **View Slide Show** mode. You can now go back and delete the speaker icon from the slide.

10. Your final presentation will be a collection of slides similar to the one shown next:

For more information online, go to:

http://www.kidzone.ws/water/

http://www.classzone.com/books/earth_science/terc/content/investigations/es0602/es0602page01.cfm

PowerPoint

BACK-TO-SCHOOL NIGHT

1

Very Easy

Project Number: PP-02

Additional hardware: None

Internet connection required? No

Template available? Yes

Grade Level: Elementary, Middle School, High School

Created by:

Teacher

Project type:

Administrative

Student learning style:

Visual

Aural

Approximate time: 30 minutes to create a 10-slide presentation

Content Area: N/A

Not Applicable

Comments: Back-to-School Night may well be the first chance you have to meet the parents of your students, and you want to make a good impression. A PowerPoint Back-to-School Night presentation will help you stay focused in your remarks and show the parents how they can best help their children have a successful school year. You can use the PowerPoint display as a key part of your presentation, or if you prefer, during teacher conferences, you can let it run in kiosk mode at the back of your room with the slides automatically advancing in a continuous loop.

Procedures: You may insert your information on the template provided on the companion CD, or you may choose to follow the procedures below.

1. Open Microsoft PowerPoint.

2. From the **Format** menu, select **Slide Design,** and choose the desired design template.

3. Go to **Slide Layout > Title Slide**. List your name, room number, grade or subject level, and any other pertinent identifying information.

4. Add slides. Select **Title, Text, and Content** slide. Make enough copies of this to allow one slide for each of things you want to address.

5. Create individual slides addressing various topics. You may want to include slides on several of the following:

   - Agenda/Items to be discussed
   - Mission statement
   - Introduce key staff
   - Introduce yourself (background, teaching philosophy)
   - Teacher expectations
   - Grading policy
   - Homework policy
   - Testing procedures
   - Classroom rules
   - Classroom management plan
   - Field trip procedures
   - Class parties (birthdays or holidays)
   - Parent volunteers/Room "Parent"
   - Parent conferences
   - Special projects
   - Schedule for the year
   - Communication with parents
   - Q & A

6. Add illustrations and custom animation as desired.

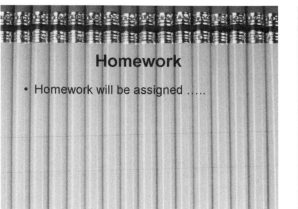

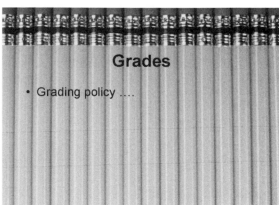

For more information online, go to:

http://www.teacherhelp.org/back_to_school.htm

Thanks to Mrs. Dawson's third-grade class for the original idea.

CLASSROOM SEATING CHART

1

Very Easy

Project Number: PP-03

Additional hardware: None

Internet connection required? No

Template available? Yes

Grade Level: Elementary, Middle School, High School

Created by:

Teacher

Project type:

Administrative

Student learning style:

Visual

Approximate time: 15 minutes to create a classroom seating chart

Content Area: **N/A**

Not Applicable

Comments: One of the many challenges in teaching is how to quickly learn the names of the many students who will pass through your doorway in the course of a school day. While this may not be too tough in an elementary school with perhaps 30 or fewer students, it becomes a bit more challenging in high school where you may have over 100 students during the various periods and classes. Seating charts provide an excellent way for you to quickly learn the names and even the faces of your students. Additionally, a seating chart allows you to quickly take attendance without wasting valuable instructional time calling roll each day, and it will prove very useful for substitute teachers.

PowerPoint

Procedures: You may insert your information on the template provided on the companion CD, or you may choose to follow the procedures below.

1. Open Microsoft PowerPoint.

2. There is no real need to select a design template, as an unadorned white background works best for this project.

3. From the **Drawing** toolbar, select **AutoShapes > Basic Shapes**.

4. Select shapes to represent furniture in the classroom: a small rectangle for student desks, a circle for round tables, a larger rectangle for teacher desks, and so on.

5. Click and drag the "student desk" shape to the approximate scaled size. Insert a **Text Box** near the desk, and type in "student name." Click and drag the cursor to select both the desk and the student name, copy and paste as many desks and names as needed, and place them about the room as represented by the PowerPoint slide. Do the same for any other needed furniture.

6. Type the actual student name in the individual **Text Boxes** in place of the generic student name.

7. Add a **Text Box** listing the class and period.

8. Select **File > Print > Print What: Slides** to get a hard copy of your work.

9. If you wish, you can even take pictures of your students with a digital camera or copied from a yearbook and insert a student photo at each desk.

10. Ready-to-use templates of several different classroom seating charts are included on the companion CD.

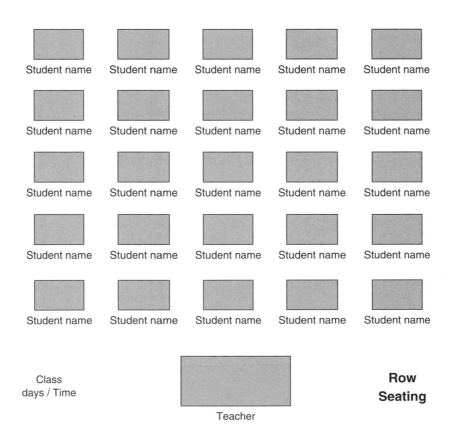

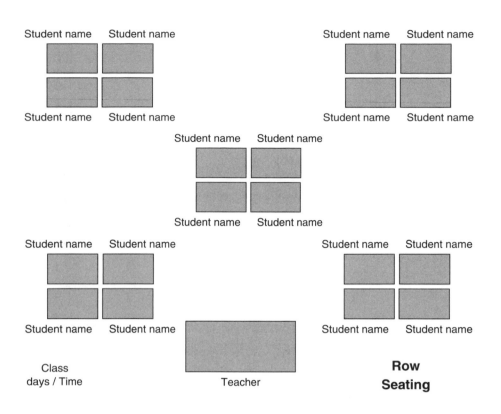

Student name   Student name

Student name   Student name

Student name   Student name

Student name   Student name

Student name   Student name

Student name   Student name

Student name   Student name

Student name   Student name

Student name   Student name

Student name   Student name

Class
days / Time

Teacher

**Row
Seating**

For more information online, go to:

http://www.edzone.net/~mwestern/tutorials.html

Power Point

POSTCARDS

Project Number:	PP-04
Additional hardware:	Scanner
Internet connection required?	No
Template available?	Yes
Grade Level:	Elementary, Middle School, High School

Very Easy

Created by:

Student and/or
Teacher

Project type:

Instructional

Student learning style:

Visual

Approximate time: 15 minutes to create one postcard

Content Area:

Language Arts

Social Studies

Comments: In this project, you will create postcards you can use to introduce yourself to the parents of your students. Students can create these also. For example, in a social studies class, students could make their own postcards with pictures of the region of interest on one side and addresses and comments on the other side. If your class has pen pals in another part of the country or world, students could create these postcards and use them to show and tell pen pals about life in your neighborhood.

Procedures: You may insert your information on the template provided on the companion CD, or you may choose to follow the procedures below.

1. Open Microsoft PowerPoint. Select **Blank Slide**.

2. Using the **AutoShapes** function or the rectangle shape on the drawing toolbar, click and drag a rectangular box to outline the entire top half of the blank slide. If the rectangle is filled, double-click within the rectangle, choose the **Colors and Lines** tab, and choose **No Fill** as the fill color.

3. Select **Line** from the drawing toolbar, and divide the large rectangle vertically into two halves. These boxes will be the front and back sides of your postcard.

4. On the "front" side, include addresses of the intended recipient, the sender, and a postage stamp, if needed.

5. On the "back" side, add text boxes with information you wish to impart to the card's recipient. Adjust the font size and style using symbols on the Standard toolbar. For introductory post-cards, you may even want to add a photo of yourself. To do this, select **Insert > Picture > From File**. Go to the proper file and select the desired picture.

6. Print the slide on heavy paper or card stock. Fold back along center line and, using double-sided tape, seal the card halves together.

7. Your completed postcard may look something like this:

Mr. Bob Smith

7th Grade History

Kennedy Middle School

Dear Parents,

It is a real pleasure for me to be working with your student this year. If you have any questions, please contact me at 555-1234 during working hours and we can arrange to meet and discuss how we can work together to best help your child have a great year!.

Sincerely, B. Smith

Mr. Bob Smith
Kennedy Middle School
123 Main Street
Kennedy, CA 94938

Place
Stamp
Here

To the Parents of:
Skippy Lou M'Darlin
543 Center Lane
Kennedy, CA 94938

For more information online, go to:

http://www.remc11.k12.mi.us/bstpract/bpIII/031/031.PDF

MATH PLACE VALUE

2

Easy

Project Number: PP-05

Additional hardware: None

Internet connection required? No

Template available? Yes

Grade Level: Elementary, Middle School

Created by:

Student and/or
Teacher

Project type:

Instructional

Student learning style:

Visual

Approximate time: 30 minutes to create a 20-slide presentation

Content Area:

Math

Comments: A proper understanding of place value is critical to developing overall number sense. Usually introduced in the early elementary years, remedial instruction in the concept of place value may continue into the middle grades and beyond. Using PowerPoint and some basic animation effects, you can enliven any lesson and have more engaged and successful students. You will undoubtedly recognize several of the state-mandated math curriculum skills being taught in this lesson.

Procedures: You may insert your information on the template provided on the companion CD, or you may choose to follow the procedures below.

1. Open Microsoft PowerPoint. After the title slide, it is probably best to select completely blank slides as you start work on this project. Begin by drawing and labeling a basic place value grid on an otherwise blank slide. Go to **Slide Sorter View** and copy and paste multiple copies of this basic slide. Make as many copies as you intend to use in sample problems.

How Many Blocks?

Hundreds	Tens	Ones

2. Select one of these blank-grid slides and add base-10 blocks to represent the desired quantities. You can create your own base-10 blocks by selecting **AutoShapes** from the Drawing Toolbar, then select **Basic Shapes**. Click and drag to form a small cube. Using the copy and the align features, you can create 10s-sticks and 100s-squares and 1,000s-cubes. Or if you prefer, you may simply cut and paste these items from the project template on the accompanying companion CD into your own presentations.

3. Now, add 100s-squares, 10s-sticks, and 1-unit blocks to the place value grid. Write the number of the units represented in each block on the lower line of the place value grid. Finally, create a text block at the bottom of the slide and enter the left side of the addition equation represented by the blocks on the place value chart. Write the answer to the equation in a second text block, to the right of the first. By so doing, you will be able to reveal the question and the answer seperately when you run the final presentation.

How Many Blocks?

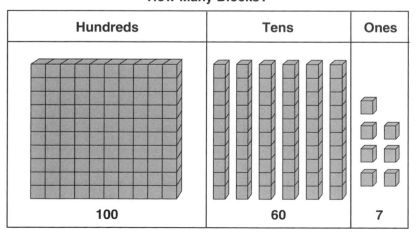

$$100 + 60 + 7 = 167$$

4. Now comes the fun part—adding the custom animation features that will bring the presentation to life! In the **Slide View** mode, go to **Slide Show > Custom Animation**. Next, click on the item in your slide you want to bring in first and select an animation effect—you have several from which to choose. Perhaps you may want to have the 100s-squares fly in first, then the 10s-sticks, followed by the 1-unit blocks. Simply select each of these in turn, add the desired animation effect, and move to the next one. You might want the items to appear in the same order you would if you were drawing them on the blackboard with chalk.

After a few examples of slides where the student is shown the number represented by the blocks, you may want to change it around some and have several numbers from which to choose. After the student has chosen what he or she believes to be the correct answer, by the click of a mouse, some marking appears on the slide to indicate the correct answer.

5. You may want to increase the number of place values by adding a 1,000s-cube.

In similar fashion, if you substitute pennies for cubes on the place value grid, you can lay the groundwork for a lesson on money.

How Many Blocks?

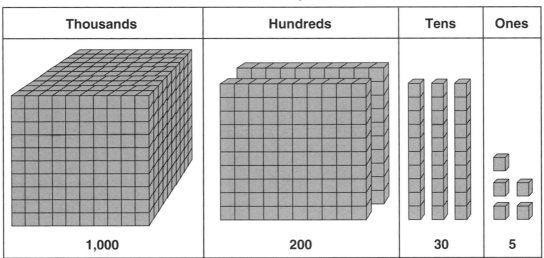

Thousands	Hundreds	Tens	Ones
1,000	200	30	5

$$1,000 + 200 + 30 + 5 = 1,235$$

6. Additional ideas using the place value grid are found on the PowerPoint presentation accompanying this lesson on the companion CD.

For more information online, go to:

http://www.eduplace.com/math/mathsteps/2/a

INSECTS

Project Number: PP-06

Additional hardware: Scanner

Internet connection required? No

Template available? Yes

Grade Level: Elementary, Middle School

Created by:
Student and/or Teacher

Project type:
Instructional

Student learning style:
Visual

Approximate time: 30 minutes to create a 10-slide presentation

Content Area:
Science

Comments: Insects have long fascinated students of all ages. What young child hasn't brought the newest captive insect into the family kitchen to proudly display to parents and siblings? Insects have their place in the world, and it is important that children understand what makes insects unique from any other members of the animal kingdom.

Procedures: You may insert your information on the template provided on the companion CD, or you may choose to follow the procedures below.

1. Open a new Microsoft PowerPoint presentation. Go to **Slide Layout** and select **Title Slide**. Name the presentation with the date and subject.

2. Add slide. Select **Title and Text** slide. Type "Insects" in the title space. Put the definition of an insect in the text space on the slide.

3. On a new slide, insert an image of an insect. Label the three primary parts of an insect (head, thorax, abdomen).

4. Label additional parts common to many insects (wings, antennae).

5. On additional slides, discuss the principle of metamorphosis. Show the four stages of development in an insect that goes through complete metamorphosis (four stages) or incomplete metamorphosis (three stages).

5. Here you can get creative. Add a picture of an insect to a blank slide. Place a blank space next to each of the parts studied. Using a new text box for each answer, write the name next to the corresponding body part. Using custom animation, you can have the answer appear when you click the mouse.

6. If you really want to be creative, add sound to each slide. This can be a sound effect for some words—the sound of a buzzing insect, or the beating of a butterfly's wings. Students may wish to add their own voice to narrate each slide in order (see Project PP-01, Water Cycle).

7. Your final presentation may be a collection of slides similar to the one shown next.

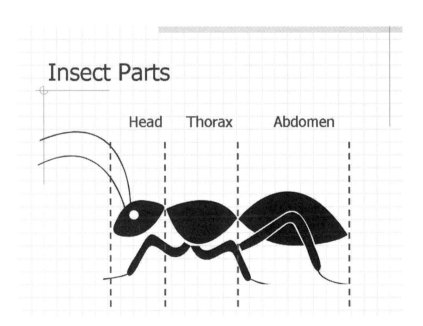

For more information online, go to:

http://www.pppst.com/index.html

SOURCE: Adapted from Ruth Petsel.

TRADING CARDS

Project Number: PP-07

Additional hardware: Scanner

Internet connection required?   No

Template available?   Yes

Grade Level: Elementary, Middle School, High School

Easy

Created by:

Student

Project type:

Instructional

Student learning style:

Visual

Approximate time: 20 minutes to create one card

Content Area:

Language Arts

Comments: Children enjoy collecting things. In this project, students will create their own trading cards to share with friends and classmates. This might make a nice introductory activity at the beginning of the school year, to help the teacher and students get acquainted. As an alternative to having students collect personal information about themselves, they could work as individuals or in teams to create a series of trading cards honoring Black History Week, early inventors, famous explorers, or U.S. presidents.

Power Point

Procedures: You may insert your information on the template provided on the companion CD, or you may choose to follow the procedures below.

1. Open Microsoft PowerPoint. Select **New Slide > Blank Slide**.

2. Draw a horizontal line, dividing the slide in half. Draw three vertical lines, evenly spaced across the slide. You should now have a total of eight rectangles.

3. Insert a photo of the child in the upper left rectangle.

4. Under the photo, add a text box with the student's name.

5. In the next space to the right, add any desired personal data like: Birthday; Favorite food, class, pet, book, and sport; and life goal.

6. Drag a box over all the text and the photo, ensuring all items are selected.

7. On the **Drawing** toolbar, select **Draw > Group**.

8. To duplicate these two rectangles (picture and data), click anywhere on the newly created group, select **Copy**, then **Paste**. Do this as often as needed to fill the slide. Drag the copies and place them in their respective squares.

9. Print the slide on heavy paper or card stock.

10. Divide the newly printed card into quarters. Fold each quarter in half again, and tape or laminate the finished card. There you have it: Instant trading cards.

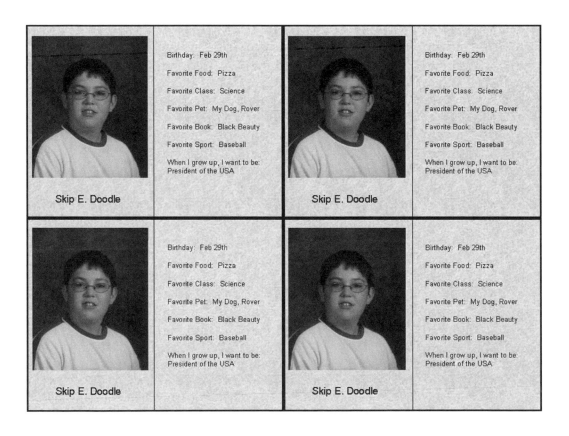

For more information online, go to:

http://www.teachers.cr.k12.de.us/~galgano/ppttradecard.doc

ANALOGIES

Easy

Project Number: PP-08

Additional hardware: None

Internet connection required? No

Template available? Yes

Grade Level: Elementary, Middle School, High School

Power Point

Created by:
Teacher

Project type:
Instructional

Student learning style:
Visual

Aural

Approximate time: 15 minutes to create a 10-slide presentation

Content Area:
Language Arts

Comments: Analogies are one way that can be used to demonstrate a student's understanding of a concept. This skill is found in most state-required curriculum standards. Additionally, analogies are a standard part of many assessment tools and are an important indicator of higher-order thinking skills. Through analogies, students can demonstrate that they understand key characteristics of a concept.

Procedures: You may insert your information on the template provided on the companion CD, or you may choose to follow the procedures below.

1. Open a new Microsoft PowerPoint presentation. Select **New Slide > Title Slide**. Name the presentation with the date and subject.

2. Add slide. Select **Title and Text** slide. Place ANALOGY in the title space. Put the definition in the text space on the slide (i.e., "two sets of words that have something in common").

3. Give several examples of analogy pairs, noting the elements they have in common.

4. Give several examples of analogy, with only three of the four words listed. Leave a blank space for the final response.

5. Here you can get creative, either by putting the answer on the next slide or by adding a separate text box with the answer in the blank space. Using custom animation, you can have the answer appear when you click the mouse.

6. If you really want to be creative, add sound to each slide. This can be a sound effect for some words—the sound of a cow "mooing" in the previous example—or you may want to add your own voice saying the analogy aloud, to help the auditory learner (see Step 8 of Project PP-01, Water Cycle).

7. Your final presentation will be a collection of slides similar to the one shown next:

Analogies are two pairs of words that have something in common.

Example:

Grass is to Green

as

Apple is to ???

The "clue" is to discover why and how the first pair go together.

- **What makes grass and green go together?**

- **The color of grass is green.**

Apple is to _____.

- **What color**
  is an apple

- **Red!**

Horse is to Bridle
as
Dog is to Leash

Hand is to Glove as
Foot is to ___

Sock

For more information online, go to:

http://www.manatee.k12.fl.us/sites/elementary/palmasola/ps3gleana.htm

Thanks to Venna Haynes for an earlier version of this project.

PowerPoint

WEATHER REPORT

2
Easy

Project Number:	PP-09
Additional hardware:	None
Internet connection required?	No
Template available?	No
Grade Level:	Elementary, Middle School

Created by:
Student

Project type:
Instructional

Student learning style:
Visual

Aural

Kinesthetic

Approximate time: 15 minutes to create a weather report

Content Area:
Science

Comments: The elements required to make up a weather report are part of the body of knowledge that all school children must master to meet most state curriculum standards. This simple, student-made presentation allows your students to demonstrate not only their presentation skills but their ability to do simple research as well. Students can be assigned to find the information and fill in the blanks in this PowerPoint presentation.

In addition to whatever other classroom jobs you have assigned to students, you may want to designate a "Class Meteorologist" to prepare this report every day for a week and have it presented to the class as part of daily announcements. This can be assigned to a single student to do daily for a period of time, or it can be assigned to teams of students with varying periods of reporting responsibility. The aural learner can hear the presentation made by class members, and the kinesthetic learner can actually go outside and note the current weather conditions. (Note: Do not allow young children to wander around outside unescorted.) For a related project, check out XL-01, Recording Weather.

PowerPoint

Procedures:

1. Have students locate the pertinent information, either by listening to radio or TV weather-casts, reading it in the newspaper, or for older students, looking it up online. This information could be collected using a worksheet, then transferred into the PowerPoint slide show at one sitting.

2. Open a new PowerPoint presentation.

3. Create a title slide.

4. Create several title and text slides, one for each of the following subjects, as desired.

   - Day/Date/Year
   - Type of day (sunny/cloudy/rainy)
   - Predicted high temperature
   - Predicted low temperature
   - Expected rainfall
   - Suggestions on what clothing might be best under the predicted conditions
   - What sorts of things might be fun to do on such a day?
   - Add any other items as needed, such as long-range forecast or any expected heavy weather or snowstorms.

5. Enter the information recorded on the worksheet in Step 1, to each of the pertinent slides.

6. Add sound effects if desired (see Step 8 of Project PP-01, Water Cycle).

7. Add custom animation if desired (see Step 7 of Project PP-01, Water Cycle).

For more information online, go to:

www.weather.com

PowerPoint

ROUNDING REVIEW

2

Easy

Project Number:	PP-10
Additional hardware:	None
Internet connection required?	No
Template available?	Yes
Grade Level:	Elementary, Middle School

Created by:

Teacher

Project type:

Instructional

Student learning style:

Visual

Aural

Approximate time: 30 minutes to create a 10-slide presentation

Content Area:

Math

Comments: Rounding numbers to the nearest 10, 100, or 1,000 often presents unique difficulties to the elementary student—sometimes even to a middle school student. Yet mastery of this skill is crucial if the student is ever going to be able to successfully approximate the costs of items or mentally complete basic consumer math problems. Using a PowerPoint presentation, you will be able to reinforce the concepts of rounding, tie into prior knowledge, and even assess student mastery of the skill. Design your own presentation by following the suggestions here, or simply modify the template on the companion CD by increasing or decreasing the number of examples accordingly.

Procedures: You may insert your information on the template provided on the companion CD, or you may choose to follow the procedures below.

1. Open a new PowerPoint Presentation, and create the title slide.

2. Go to Microsoft clips online and download a picture of a frog.

3. Draw a portion of the number line, numbers 30 through 40, at least 10 digits long. Place the frog above the Number 35, with a caption reading "Round 35 to the nearest 10."

4. On the next slide, copy the number line. This time, place the frog over the Number 40, with the caption reading "35 rounds to 40 because 5 or more rounds to the next higher 10."

5. Using different sections of the number line, give similar examples, repeating the rule used in rounding for the first few pairs of slides.

6. Next, eliminate the number line and have the frog simply ask rounding questions; answer them in the next slide, repeating the rule used to get the answer.

7. For the final set of problems, have the frog ask the questions, and have the students answer, without the frog restating the rule. Have the answer revealed in sequence, using custom animation to have the question and answer disclosed sequentially.

For more information online, go to:

http://www.aaamath.com/est27a-rounding.html

SOURCE: Adapted from an earlier version by Richard Fitzgerald.

PowerPoint

VOCABULARY WORDS FLASH CARDS

Project Number:	PP-11
Additional hardware:	None
Internet connection required?	No
Template available?	Yes
Grade Level:	Elementary, Middle School, High School

3
Medium Difficulty

Created by:
Student and/or Teacher

Project type:
Instructional

Student learning style:
Visual   Aural

Approximate time: 45 minutes to create a 10-card set

Content Area:
Language Arts   Math   Science   Social Studies

Comments: Many state departments of education have required vocabulary words for different grade levels. Certainly, each of the disciplines has specific terminology the student must understand in order to master the subject matter. To find out if your state has required vocabulary lists, check out the State Educational Agency Web Sites listed in supplementary Resource C.

This project helps students learn their vocabulary words or math facts using a multimodal approach—teaching the selected words using sights (images and symbols) and sounds appealing to both the visual and the auditory learner. Unlike the Microsoft Word Flash Cards (WD-17) in the previous chapter, these PowerPoint flash cards can incorporate animation and sounds to further solidify the learning.

Procedures: You may insert your information on the template provided on the companion CD, or you may choose to follow the procedures below.

1. Open Microsoft PowerPoint.

2. Go to **Slide Layout** and select **Title Slide.** Name the presentation with the date and subject.

3. Add slide. Select a **Title, Text, and Content** slide. Make enough copies of this to allow one slide for each of the assigned vocabulary words.

4. On each slide, print the desired vocabulary word in the title section, the definition in the text section, and insert an image, photograph, or clipart that illustrates the word in the content section. For example, if the vocabulary word is *cow*, you might include a picture of a cow.

5. ADDING SOUND: If you really want to be creative, add sound to each slide. This can be a sound effect for some words—the sound of a cow "mooing" in the previous example—or you may want to add your own voice pronouncing and/or even spelling the word orally.

   a. To add sound, find the sound you want from the Internet, a sound effects CD, or other source. Make sure it is a .wav sound file, since PowerPoint cannot easily use file types with different extensions like .mp3, among others. Store this sound file in an easily locatable place on your computer.

   b. From the drop-down menu at the top of the screen, select **Insert > Movies and Sounds > Sound from File**. Navigate to the desired file and select **OK**.

   c. Decide whether you want the sound to play automatically when you first open the slide or play only when clicked.

6. Go to the drop-down menu at the top of the screen. Select **Slide Show > Custom Animation.** Individually select each of the items on your slide and decide how you want them to enter during the presentation (One letter at a time? Entire word? Entire sentence?) In what order do you want the items to appear? Do you want the word, definition, image, or sound to appear first?

7. For initial instruction, you may want the word to appear first, followed by the definition. For review, however, you may want to show the definition first and have the student give the word. Having the definition follow the word will provide immediate feedback to the student during group or independent practice.

8. Your final presentation will be a collection of slides similar to the one shown next.

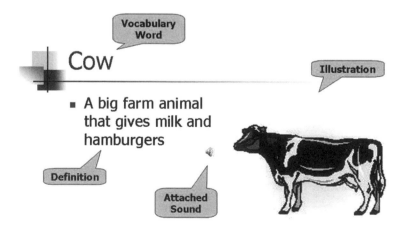

For more information online, go to:

http://www.merriamwebster.com

Q & A Review

Project Number:	PP-12
Additional hardware:	None
Internet connection required?	No
Template available?	Yes
Grade Level:	Elementary, Middle School, High School

Medium Difficulty

Created by:

Teacher

Project type:

Instructional

Student learning style:

Visual

Approximate time: 30 minutes to create a 20-question review

Content Area:

Language Arts

Math

Science

Social Studies

Comments: Teachers are constantly on the lookout for interesting ways to review material addressed in class. Using PowerPoint, you can create simple question-and-answer format slides to cover all manner of topics.

Procedures: You may insert your information on the template provided on the companion CD, or you may choose to follow the procedures below.

1. Open a new Microsoft PowerPoint presentation. Select **Slide Layout > Title Slide** and enter presentation title information.

2. Select **Slide Layout > Title and Text**. In the content section, type the word *Question*, skip down two lines, and type the word *Answer*.

3. On the toolbar, select **Slide Show > Custom Animation.** Click on the the word ***Question*** in the content area and select the desired animation mode.

4. Go to **Slide Sorter View**. Copy the Q&A slide, then paste as many slides as needed for the full presentation.

5. Return to the beginning of the content slides and enter pairs of actual questions and answers on each slide.

6. The completed slides may look similar to these:

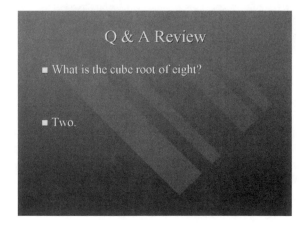

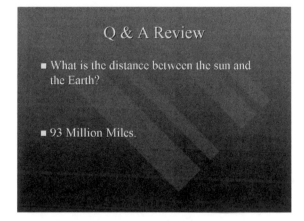

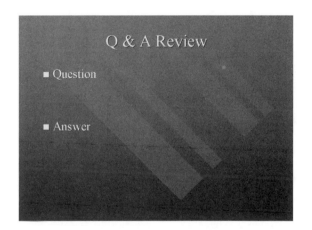

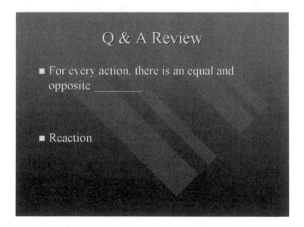

PowerPoint

ELECTRONIC PORTFOLIO

Medium Difficulty

Project Number: PP-13

Additional hardware: Scanner

Internet connection required? No

Template available? Yes

Grade Level: Elementary, Middle School, High School

Created by:

Student

Project type:

Administrative

Student learning style:

Visual

Approximate time: 60 minutes to create a 10-slide presentation

Content Area:

Language Arts

Math

Science

Social Studies

Comments: The electronic portfolio is an excellent way for students to showcase the work they have done in your classroom. Using this student-created PowerPoint presentation, you will have a concise and interesting way to document student performance. The students will enjoy selecting some of their best work to showcase, and you will have an effective tool for use in parent conferences or open house nights to demonstrate what your students have accomplished. Increasingly, portfolio assessments are being used to document performance of students with special learning needs. This electronic portfolio could possibly be used as a part of state-mandated assessments.

Procedures: You may insert your information on the template provided on the companion CD, or you may choose to follow the procedures below.

1. Collect several examples of a student's work. Ensure you have representative pieces from all the selected academic areas.

2. Using a flatbed scanner, scan samples of student work and save them as JPEG or BMP files. NOTE: When scanning and saving documents, be certain the file sizes do not exceed a few hundred kilobytes, lest the finished product become too large and unmanageable.

3. Open a new Microsoft PowerPoint presentation. Select the **Title Slide** from the slide layout selections. Add an appropriate title for the presentation, including student name, teacher name, date, and subjects as needed.

4. Add a new, blank slide. Include a Table of Contents list of all the other pages to be included in the presentation (e.g., math, social studies, language arts, science, etc.).

5. Add blank slides for each of the areas listed on the opening slide. Include slides for pages titled "My Strengths," "Improvement Goals," and "Parent Focus."

6. Insert the scanned images of student work onto the appropriate pages.

7. Hyperlink each page to its corresponding entry on the Table of Contents slide. Highlight the entry on the Table of Contents slide. Right Click and select **Hyperlink > Place in This Document**. Select the desired page to which you want to link. Repeat the process for each item listed in the Table of Contents.
NOTE: The hyperlink will work only when you are in the Slideshow mode. It will not work in the Normal mode used to create the original slides.

8. Next, you will need a way to get quickly back to the Table of Contents page from anywhere in the portfolio. On one of the content pages, draw a small box in a lower corner. Select this box and hyperlink it to the Table of Contents page following the procedures in Step 7 above. Add "To Contents" in the box. Next, copy and paste this box onto all the other slides in the presentation.

9. The finished product may have the following basic slides, augmented as your circumstances dictate.

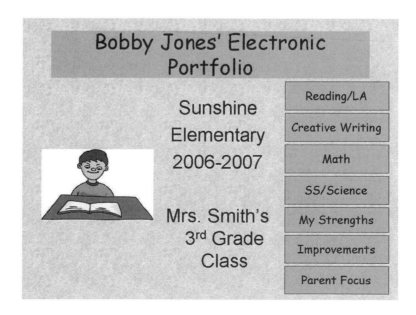

PowerPoint

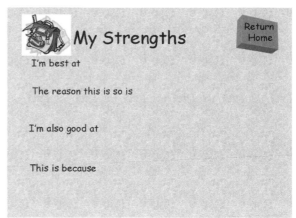

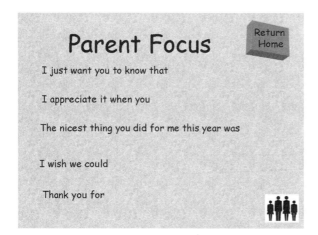

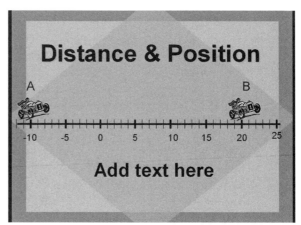

For more information online, go to:

http://www.uvm.edu/~jmorris/ePortquest/ePortfolioquestresources.html

Thanks to Lisa Andry for an earlier version of this project.

COMPARING NUMBERS

Project Number:	PP-14
Additional hardware:	None
Internet connection required?	No
Template available?	Yes
Grade Level:	Elementary, Middle School

3

Medium Difficulty

Created by:

Teacher

Project type:

Instructional

Student learning style:

Visual

Approximate time: 30 minutes to create a 10-slide presentation

Content Area:

Math

Comments: Comparing numbers, and the concepts of "greater than" or "less than" are critical skills in developing number sense for young students. Using the Place Value Grid developed in Project PP-05, you will be able to graphically portray two numbers of different value on the same slide and have the student make comparisons. Later, you will be able to work with just the numbers alone, and students will be able to make the same comparisons.

Power Point

Procedures: You may insert your information on the template provided on the companion CD, or you may choose to follow the procedures below.

1. Create a place value grid and divide it with a horizontal line into two sections. Display two sets of blocks in the different columns. After students have identified the numerical values represented in each half of the grid, display the numbers next to or below each group. Have the students make comparisons between the two groups.

Compare?

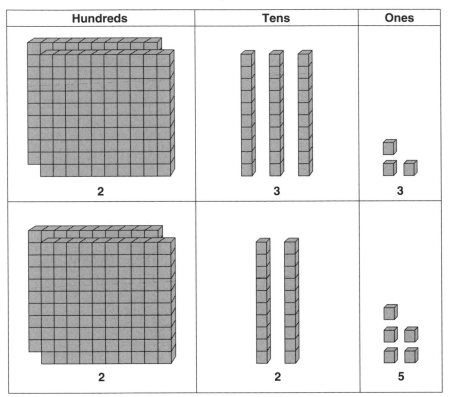

Hundreds	Tens	Ones
2	3	3
2	2	5

2. On the next slide, place the two numbers representing the blocks on the previous slide. Add the greater than sign (>) or the less than symbol sign (<) between the two numbers. Go to **Slide Show**, then **Custom Animation**. Click on the > symbol, and pick an entering effect.

Compare

233 > 225

3. When you play the slide show, each part can be entered selectively. Create several pairs of slides to demonstrate the idea. Eventually, you should stop making companion slides with the blocks and just have students compare two numbers.

WHERE I LIVE

Project Number:	PP-15
Additional hardware:	Scanner
Internet connection required?	Yes
Template available?	Yes
Grade Level:	Elementary, Middle School

Medium Difficulty

PowerPoint

Created by:

Student and/or Teacher

Project type:

Instructional

Student learning style:

Visual

Approximate time: 30 minutes to create a 10-slide presentation

Content Area:

Social Studies

Comments: Young children are often bewildered by the concept of location, confusing the differences between community, town, state, nation, continent, and hemisphere. This is an easy-to-create presentation that will help a child visualize these interrelationships.

Procedures: You may insert your information on the template provided on the companion CD, or you may choose to follow the procedures below.

1. Open a new Microsoft Powerpoint presentation.

2. Select **Title Slide** and enter name of presentation and class information.

3. Select a new **Title and Content** slide. Make five copies of this slide.

4. On the title line of these five slides, place the words "My Neighborhood," "My Town" (or city), "My State," "My Country," "My Continent," "My Hemisphere," and "My World," respectively.

5. In the content area of each slide, place an image of the appropriate area. These images can be scanned pictures or images downloaded from the Internet and placed in a picture file created for this purpose. Use a star symbol to indicate the student's home on each map.

6. Your final presentation may include slides that look something like this:

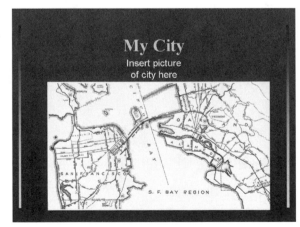

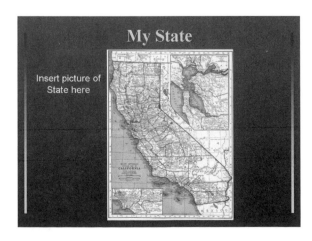

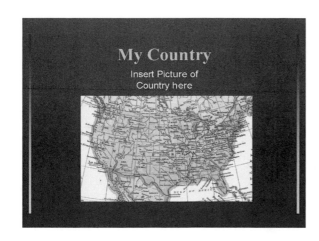

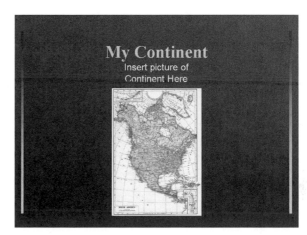

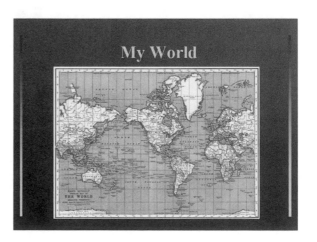

For more information online, go to:

www.mapquest.com

PowerPoint

MULTIPLE-CHOICE TEST

Difficult

Project Number:	PP-16
Additional hardware:	None
Internet connection required?	No
Template available?	Yes
Grade Level:	Elementary, Middle School, High School

Created by:
Teacher

Project type:
Instructional

Student learning style:
Visual

Aural

Approximate time: 30 minutes to create a 10-slide test

Content Area:
Language Arts

Math

Science

Social Studies

Comments: PowerPoint can offer a unique way to assess student learning. Using the sound features of this software to reinforce correct responses, students will receive immediate feedback on their answers. This particular project may prove useful in student self-assessments.

Procedures: You may insert your information on the template provided on the companion CD, or you may choose to follow the procedures below.

1. Open a new Microsoft PowerPoint presentation. Select **Title Slide**, and enter test identifying data.

2. Use either a sound effects file or download from the Internet the sounds of a crowd applauding and of a bell clanging once.

3. Select **New Slide** and choose the **Title and 2-Column** slide. Make one slide for each intended test question.

4. Type the test questions in the title section of each slide. Place two possible answers in each of the two column sections, for a total of four possible answers per slide.

5. On each slide, insert the two sound effects you downloaded. When you insert a sound, a small icon shaped like a speaker will appear in the center of the slide. When you click on these icons, they will play their respective sounds. Copy and paste the **Bell** sound effect three times for each slide. Paste the **Applause** sound effect only once per slide. Move these small sound icons around until you have one icon in front of each of the four possible answers, making sure the **Applause** Icon is in front of the correct response.

6. Your finished slide show will look something like this:

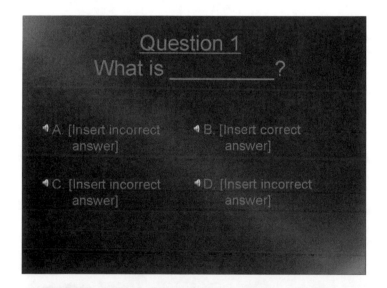

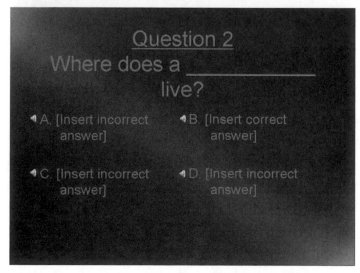

PowerPoint

TALKING BOOK

5
Very Difficult

Project Number: PP-17

Additional hardware: None

Internet connection required? No

Template available? Yes

Grade Level: Elementary, Middle School, High School

Created by:
Student and/or Teacher

Project type:
Instructional

Student learning style:
Visual

Aural

Approximate time: 150 minutes to create a seven-page talking book

Content Area:
Language Arts

Science

Social Studies

Comments: Of all the projects listed in this book, the Talking Book is arguably one of the most involved, combining scanned images, downloaded sound effects, recorded student voices, and PowerPoint animation to create a true multimedia product. These talking books will energize any language arts curriculum. Talking books can be used for introductory or remedial reading instruction. They can be used to develop higher-order thinking skills as the students synthesize information presented to make predictions about the stories. Social studies curriculum can be brought to life as students develop their own multimedia projects describing events of historic signifigance. Plan to allow a couple of class periods for this project. The results will be worth the effort!

You do not need to scan dozens of pages to make an effective talking book. After using just a few pages from the beginning of the story, you can have your students identify themes and characters and make predictions about how the story will turn out. Or you may want your students to make up their own illustrations and text to complete the story. These student-made illustrations could be scanned and added to the talking book. Samples of student-made talking books are included on the companion CD.

NOTE: Please review the Fair Use and Copyright section at the end of Chapter 1 prior to scanning pictures from materials that are copyright protected.

Procedures: You may insert your information on the template provided on the companion CD, or you may choose to follow the procedures below.

1. The teacher or student should select a favorite illustrated children's book from the school library or from home. Scan the cover and about six to eight pictures, saving them to a designated file. Be certain when scanning images that you reduce the resolution and/or image size to keep the file sizes manageable. Try to limit scanned images to no larger than 300 kb in size. If the file size is too large, adding several of these pictures into a presentation may make the final project too big to move around easily.

2. Open Microsoft PowerPoint. Stay with a **Blank Slide** layout for this project. You can go back and experiment with different backgrounds later. Copy and paste seven or eight blank pages to begin your presentation.

3. ADDING IMAGES: For each slide, go to the pull-down menu near the top of the screen, select **Insert > Picture > From File** and navigate to the file where you stored your scanned images. Beginning with the scanned front cover, insert one picture per page until all scanned images have been included. At this point, you may go back and select a suitable background for each slide by going to **Format** on the drop-down menu at the top of the screen and selecting **Background**.

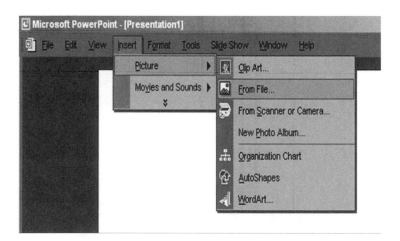

4. ADDING WRITTEN TEXT: Depending on the layout of the original book, the text may have been scanned along with the illustration. If the text was on an opposite page, simply add a text box and type in the words that go with that illustration. If it is hard to read the text against a multicolored background, you can select a pastel color fill for your text box.

5. ADDING SOUND EFFECTS: You may want to enhance the effectiveness of the image a bit by selecting a sound effect, audio clip, or short musical piece that will play as you view a certain page. Sound effects can be located and downloaded using any of the larger search engines (Google.com or Altavista.com, for example). PowerPoint is designed to work best with sound effects that carry the .wav extention. You may locate some really effective sound effects, but if they are .mp3 or other formats, PowerPoint may not recognize them as legitimate audio files.

6. ADDING SPOKEN TEXT: You and your students will have fun with this part, as they become junior recording artists. To record spoken words, you will need a pin jack or USB plug microphone. These mics can be found for a reasonable price (usually $20.00 or less) at office supply stores or computer centers.

   a. Select the desired slide, being sure you are in the **Normal View** mode. From the pull-down menu at the top of the screen select **Insert > Movies and Sounds > Record Sounds.**

   b. The default name listed on the window that appears is **Recorded Sound**. Replace this name with one of your own choosing, but make it unique to that particular slide. Position the **Record Sound** window so it doesn't cover the text you want to read. Press the red-circle record button, wait one second, read the desired text, wait one second, push the blue-rectangle stop button. Pressing the blue-triangle playback button will allow you to review what you have just recorded.

   c. If you like what you hear, press **OK** to save your recording and move on to the next slide. A small speaker icon will appear in the center of the slide. You can click and drag this icon anywhere you want on the slide. By clicking on this icon while in **View Slide Show** mode, you should hear the recorded audio clip. If you want the sound clip to play automatically, go to the **Slide Sorter View** and select **Slide Transition**. At this point, locate the word **Sound** and click on the pull-down menu. Find and select the desired sound file. This sound should now play automatically when you come to the slide in the **View Slide Show** mode. You can now go back and delete the speaker icon from the slide.

7. AUTOMATIC SLIDE ADVANCE: You may want your slide show to run in a fully automatic mode. To make this happen, select **Slide Show** > **Rehearse Timings**.

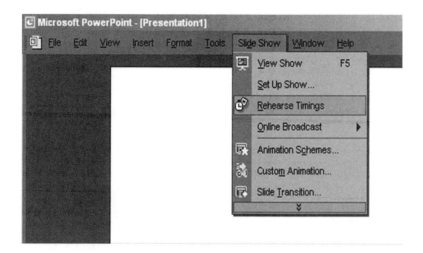

a. Your first slide will appear and any attached sound clip should play. After what you deem a suitable interval, perhaps after the narration or sound effect is completed, manually advance to the next slide using the down arrow on your keyboard. After another suitable interval, continue advancing through the entire show until you reach the end.

b. You will see a screen that gives the total time for your slide show, and asks if you want to keep the slide show timings. Select **Yes**.

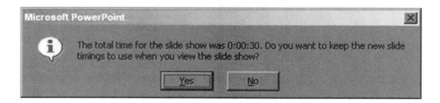

8. You should now be able to view your fully automated talking book on any suitably configured computer running the same version of PowerPoint or newer.

For more information online, go to:

http://atto.buffalo.edu/registered/Tutorials/talkingBooks/ppt_ace.pdf

Thanks to Rita Edmundson and Christie Tickell for the sample projects PP-17a and PP-17b on the companion CD.

WEBQUEST

5

Very Difficult

Project Number:	PP-18
Additional hardware:	None
Internet connection required?	Yes
Template available?	Yes
Grade Level:	Elementary, Middle School

Created by:

Student and/or Teacher

Project type:

Instructional

Student learning style:

Visual

Aural

Approximate time: 120 minutes to create a 15-slide presentation

Content Area:

Science

Social Studies

Comments: Perhaps one of the more challenging PowerPoint presentations to design, the WebQuest also has the potential to be one of the most dynamic and interactive, as well as having the greatest instructional value to students, of any of the projects presented in this book. The project can be designed to cover a single class period or an entire thematic unit over several class sessions. A WebQuest can combine PowerPoint, Internet Scavenger Hunt, and Talking Book into a single, comprehensive project. It can be teacher generated to assess mastery of a subject. An even better use for WebQuest might be as a team project, with individual students responsible for specific portions of the finished project.

Procedures: You may insert your information on the template provided on the companion CD, or you may choose to follow the procedures below.

1. Open a new Microsoft PowerPoint presentation.

2. Select **Title Slide**. Add presentation title. For this example, we will use the Roman Empire as the topic of this WebQuest.

3. Select **Title and Content** slide. Create a Table of Contents. Each topic listed in the Table of Contents should be hyperlinked to the appropriate slide in the presentation so that the reader can point the cursor at the desired topic, click the mouse, and be jumped to the desired page (see Step 7 of PP-13, Electronic Portfolio).

4. Each specific page of the WebQuest should address a different aspect of the project. For this example, you could design different slides in your PowerPoint presentation to address different aspects of Ancient Rome. You could have slides that address the Roman army, Roman battle tactics, the culture of Rome, Roman gods, the extent of the Roman Empire, and the fall of the Roman Empire. On each of these slides, place information about that specific aspect of the Roman Empire.

5. In the bottom corner of each slide, place a small object (known as a button) that will hyperlink you back to the Table of Contents slide. You can draw a small box or any other closed figure. Add the words "To Contents" in this box. Right Click on this box and select **Hyperlink > Place in This Document**. Select the slide that contains the Table of Contents to which you want to link.

6. Additionally, you can add to each slide a hyperlink to an Internet Web site where the reader can find out more information about the topic of the slide. Include links to children's games and other interesting information about Ancient Rome.

7. As part of the lesson, you can include slides with questions for students to answer and problems for them to solve, either alone or in groups. Include an information scavenger hunt, with hyperlinks to sites that contain clues to help answer the questions.

8. A Web site devoted to WebQuests has several excellent examples of WebQuests either as a source for ideas or as a location to get WebQuests ready for classroom use.

For more information online, go to:

http://webquest.org/

PowerPoint

PowerPoint

PSEUDO-JEOPARDY QUIZ GAME

5

Very Difficult

Project Number: PP-19

Additional hardware: None

Internet connection required?   No

Template available?   No

Grade Level: Elementary, Middle School, High School

Created by:
Student and/or Teacher

Project type:
Instructional

Student learning style:
Visual

Aural

Approximate time: 150 minutes to create one, 30-question game

Content Area:
Language Arts

Math

Science

Social Studies

Comments: Jeopardy is one of the most popular television game shows of all time. It has been made available in many different languages and mediums and is enjoyed by audiences of all ages. Now it is available for classroom use in any subject or grade level. Developing your own Jeopardy Game from the ground up may be a rather complicated and time-consuming task, but there are many templates available on the Internet where that work has been already done for you. The one used here was created by Matt Hamlyn. You simply fill in your own questions and answers on the designated slides in the template included on the companion CD, and soon you will have a valuabe tool for use in classroom instruction or assessment of material already learned. You may even decide to have your students generate the questions and answers to use in a game, as a way of determining prior knowledge when beginning a new unit. Or student-generated material could make a fun way to conduct an end-of-unit review.

Procedures:

1. Several different versions of the game can be downloaded from the Internet, each with slight differences in the number and quality of the added features. Some have special slides for keeping a running total of points earned; others include different sound and visual effects. Some versions allow for only one round of questions (30 questions total, 60+ slides). Other versions include a second, Double Jeopardy round, allowing for up to 60 questions and a Final Jeopardy question (over 125 slides). Typing the words "Jeopardy PowerPoint Game" into most Internet search engines will return thousands of Web sites where these games may be found and downloaded.

2. Feel free to make changes in the basic rules of play. For instance, younger children may be confused when presented with the answer first, where they must "phrase their statement in the form of a question." Older students, on the other hand, may have no trouble with this. However, if you do one on mathematics, it might be best if you give the question first, since a single answer in math may be a valid answer for any number of questions. You know your students best and can decide whether you want to reveal the question or the answer first.

3. You may want to list your questions and answers on paper first, before typing them into the slides. Identify six categories and develop five questions for each category. Arrange your questions and answers in order from simple to complex and place them on the appropriately annotated slides, with the more complex questions worth more.

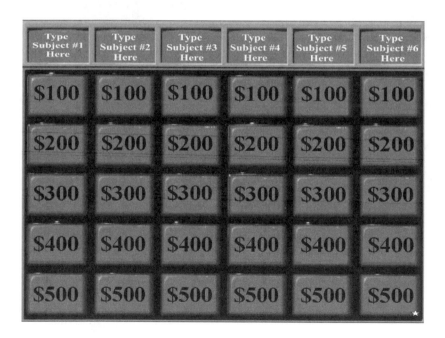

For more information online, go to:

http://www.ucvts.tec.nj.us/ucvts/ETTC/Resources/Powerpoint%20Templates/_body

Thanks to Matt Hamlyn for the original version of this.

PowerPoint

CRITICAL READING FOR CONTENT

Very Difficult 5

Project Number: PP-20

Additional hardware: None

Internet connection required? No

Template available?   Yes

Grade Level: Elementary, Middle School, High School

Created by:

Teacher

Project type:

Instructional

Student learning style:

Visual

Approximate time: 45 minutes to create a three-question presentation

Content Area:

Language Arts

Science

Social Studies

Comments: This project is fairly ambitious and will take some time to set up, but the results can be well worth it. It will make a good addition to your "instructional toolkit." Through the liberal use of slide-to-slide hyperlinks, this can be used to develop a student's ability to glean important information from a passage of text. While primarily a language arts project, this same project may be used to teach science or social studies content as well. For the purposes of this exercise, I have chosen a passage from the Gettysburg Address.

Procedures: You may insert your information on the template provided on the companion CD, or you may choose to follow the procedures below.

1. Open a new Microsoft PowerPoint presentation.

2. Select **Title Slide** and enter title.

3. Select **Blank Slide** (All entries on these slides will be made using **Text Box**).

4. Create slides with the words "Correct – Keep Going" and "Oops – Go Back and Try again" on them, respectively.

5. Enter the source text used for the first series of questions, as in the next example:

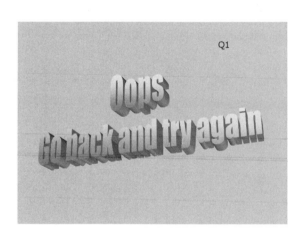

Gettysburg Address Q1

Read the following passage from the speech, "The Gettysburg Address"

"Four score and seven years ago our fathers brought forth on this continent, a new nation, conceived in Liberty, and dedicated to the proposition that all men are created equal. Now we are engaged in a great civil war, testing whether that nation, or any nation so conceived and so dedicated, can long endure. We are met on a great battle-field of that war. We have come to dedicate a portion of that field, as a final resting place for those who here gave their lives that that nation might live. It is altogether fitting and proper that we should do this. "

Place reading passage here

6. Select another **Blank Slide**. Enter the first question and four possible answers.

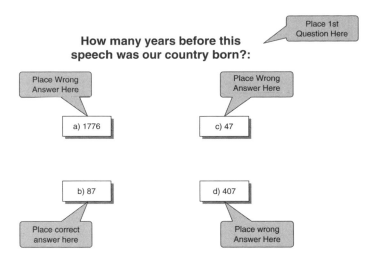

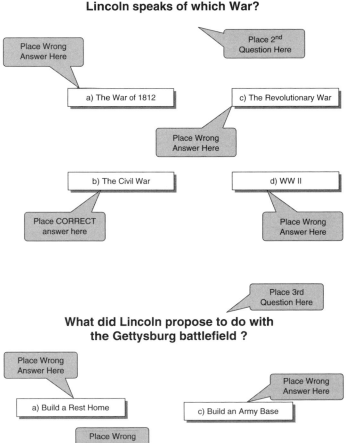

7. Right click each one of the four possible answers. Select **Hyperlink**. Select **Place in this document**. Select either the "Correct – Keep Going" or the "Incorrect – Try Again" slide created earlier, depending on the answer selected. When in the **Slide Show** mode, clicking on the answer should cause you to jump to the desired next slide.

8. Create a final slide, indicating completion of the entire section. Link the correct answer of the last question to this slide.

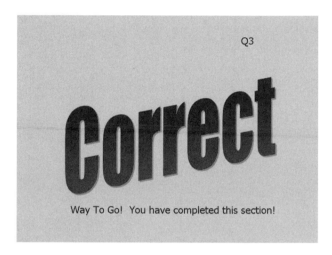

9. The sample PowerPoint project on the enclosed companion CD contains a sample of text and three questions about the text. You may substitute the sample text and questions with those of your own choosing. Additional passages and questions may be added as desired, once you have mastered the basics of hyperlinking.

For more information online, go to:

http://www.criticalreading.com/critical_reading.htm

4

Microsoft Excel Projects

In this chapter you will find the following activities:

Project Number	Title	Difficulty	Created By
XL-01	Recording Weather	2	Student and/or Teacher
XL-02	Peer Grading Rubric	2	Teacher
XL-03	Class Grade Book	3	Teacher
XL-04	Self-Checking Quiz	3	Teacher
XL-05	Skeletal System	3	Teacher
XL-06	Five in a Row	3	Teacher
XL-07	Annotated Family Tree	3	Student
XL-08	Measures of Central Tendency	3	Student and/or Teacher
XL-09	Ratios, Fractions, Decimals, Percentages	3	Teacher
XL-10	Counting Coins	4	Teacher
XL-11	Math Four-Function Worksheets	4	Teacher
XL-12	Interactive Map	4	Student and/or Teacher
XL-13	Practice With Multiplication	5	Teacher

INTRODUCTION TO MICROSOFT EXCEL

Microsoft Excel is a program that lets you create your own spreadsheets. A spreadsheet is nothing more than a rectangular information grid. The cells on a spreadsheet are arranged in horizontal rows and vertical columns. The real magic of Excel is in the makeup of the cell. You can change the color, shape, size, content, and function of the cell and even attach a comment box to a cell. Manipulating cell data can lead to all sorts of learning experiences. Information is entered into various cells where it can be ordered and processed. Financial or other numerical data entered into the spreadsheet can be manipulated using built-in formulas, and solutions to problems can be generated automatically by the computer. Spreadsheets are used extensively in the business world to keep track of budgets and the like, but Excel is becoming increasingly popular in the classroom as a manipulator of textual information as well.

Some people are not aware of the versatility of Excel spreadsheets, focusing only on the math manipulation capabilities of the program and ignoring other uses. This may be particularly true among teachers and students who harbor a secret distaste for all things mathematical. But to discount the benefits of Excel is a mistake, for as the examples included on the companion CD demonstrate, Excel can prove to be the program of choice in many classrooms in improving student achievement.

Excel can have many classroom applications. Suggested projects include making self-correcting quizzes (in all content areas, not just math), labeling multipart diagrams of the skeletal system or of the United States, even generating a family tree or a sports tournament bracket tracking your school team in the district athletic league. You can even make self-scoring rubrics for peer editing.

RECORDING WEATHER

Project Number: XL-01

Additional hardware: None

Internet connection required? No

Template available? Yes

Grade Level: Elementary, Middle School, High School

2
Easy

Created by:
Student and/or
Teacher

Project type:
Instructional

Student learning style:
Visual

Kinesthetic

Approximate time: 30 minutes to create a one-month weather spreadsheet

Content Area:
Science

Comments: Early elementary students are taught to make observations about the world around them. Among these are observations about the weather. By collecting these observations, students can begin to make predictions about the weather to complement the observations. Using the features of Microsoft Excel, you can create a spreadsheet that will automatically record the total number of occurrences of a given weather type, as well as note minimum, maximum, and average temperatures. For a related project, see Project PP-09, Today's Weather.

Procedures:

1. Open Project XL-01 on the companion CD included with this book.

2. Customize the spreadsheet by entering the name of the desired month in Cell F1.

3. Next, add the days of the week and corresponding dates in Columns B and C.

4. Have students note daily weather observations by placing an X (or any other symbol you choose) in the appropriate category for each day. Excel will automatically convert the mark to the number 1 and add them at the bottom of the column.

5. The program will keep track of how many of each day were observed in Row 36—Totals

6. Have students record the high and low temperatures noted during the school day. The Excel spreadsheet will automatically track the maximum and minimum temperatures for the month, as well as determine the average temperature for the month.

7. Students can compare their recorded observations of highs, lows, and average temperatures with those predicted by the National Weather Service and with historical records of the areas.

		The Weather			December, 200X				
Type									
Totals		0	0	0	0	0	0	0	0
Day	Date	Sunny	Partly Cloudy	Cloudy	Rainy	Snowy	Windy	Hi Temp	Lo Temp
Sunday	15								
Monday	16								
Tuesday	17								
Wednesday	18								
Thursday	19								
Friday	20								
Saturday	21								
Sunday	22								
Monday	23								
Tuesday	24								
Wednesday	25								
Thursday	26								
Friday	27								
Saturday	28								
Sunday	29								
Monday	30								
Tuesday	31								
Totals		0	0	0	0	0	0		
Maximum Temp	0		Minimum Temp	0		Average Temp	#DIV/0!		

For more information online, go to:

http://atm.geo.nsf.gov/instruction/observations.html

Thanks to Amy Ramsey for an earlier version of this project.

PEER GRADING RUBRIC

2

Easy

Project Number: XL-02

Additional hardware: None

Internet connection required? No

Template available? Yes

Grade Level: Elementary, Middle School, High School

Created by:

Teacher

Project type:

Instructional

Student learning style:

Visual

Aural

Approximate time: 30 minutes to create a 4″ × 6″ rubric

Content Area:

Language Arts

Science

Social Studies

Comments: Rubrics are becoming an increasingly popular tool for grading student work. Properly designed, rubrics can serve not only as an assessment tool but as an aid to instruction by indicating the required standards of excellence in each of several areas. Rubrics can help students understand the differences between substandard, mediocre, good, and excellent projects and written assignments. By having peers grade each other's work, you have the added benefit of students reviewing assignments other than their own and exercising higher-order thinking skills of analysis and compare and contrast. For an example of a similar rubric using Access instead of Excel, see Project AC-14, Peer Review.

Excel

Procedures:

1. Rather than create a new rubric from scratch, it may be easier to modify the rubric on the companion CD as needed for the specific project being evaluated. That example, shown below, is designed for evaluating written work.

Criteria	4 Point	3 Point	2 Point	1 Point	
Topic Sentence	Each paragraph starts with a well-constructed and focused topic sentence.	Almost all paragraphs start with a well-constructed topic sentence.	The topic sentences are not well constructed and they don't focus on one topic.	Paragraphs do not start with a sentence with a focused topic.	
	○ Excellent 4 Points	◉ Good – 3 Points	○ Fair – 2 Points	○ Poor – 1 Point	3
Supporting Details	Each paragraph contains 2 or 3 details that support the topic.	Each paragraph contains at least 2 details that support the topic.	Each paragraph contains at least 1 detail that supports the topic.	Paragraphs do not contain details that support the topic.	
	○ Excellent – 4 Points	○ Good – 3 Points	○ Fair – 2 Points	◉ Poor – 1 Point	1
Vocabulary	Vivid words and phrases are used that bring the topic alive and are used accurately.	Vivid words and phrases are used that bring the topic alive and they may not always be used accurately.	The vocabulary words used clearly communicate ideas but there is a lack of variety	The vocabulary used is limited and does not adequately communicate ideas.	
	◉ Excellent – 4 Points	○ Good – 3 Points	○ Fair – 2 Points	○ Poor – 1 Point	4
Grammar & Spelling	There are no errors in grammar or spelling.	There are 1 or 2 errors in grammar or spelling but they don't affect meaning.	There are 3 or 4 errors in grammar or spelling that distract the reader from the content.	There are more than 4 errors in grammar or spelling that make the paper difficult to understand.	
	○ Excellent – 4 PointsP.	◉ Good – 3 Points	○ Fair – 2 Points	○ Poor – 1 Point	3
Capitalization & Punctuation	There are no errors in capitalization or punctuation.	There are 1 or 2 errors in capitalization and/or punctuation but the paper is still easy to understand.	There are a few errors in capitalization and/or punctuation that distracts from the content.	There are more than 4 errors in capitalization and/or punctuation that make the paper difficult to understand.	
	◉ Excellent – 4 Points	○ Good – 3 Points	○ Fair – 2 Points	○ Poor – 1 Point	4
Conclusion	The conclusion is well constructed and draws together all the details to form an ending.	There is a conclusion and it draws together most of the details.	There is a conclusion but it doesn't draw together most of the details.	There is no clear conclusion or ending to the paper.	
	○ Excellent – 4 Points	◉ Good – 3 Points	○ Fair – 2 Points	○ Poor – 1 Point	3
				Total Score	**18**

2. Note that the point values corresponding to the option buttons selected appear in the right-hand column. The mathematical calculations are already integrated into the basic spreadsheet. The total scores possible on the sample rubric range from 6 to 24 points.

3. This template can be modified as needed to evaluate other forms of work by substituting cell values as desired. The example given is used to evaluate a language arts presentation. To create your own rubric for a class of your choosing, it is best to first draw a four-column grid on a piece of paper where you can rough out your ideas before transferring them to the template provided.

4. Creating a rubric involves the following steps:
   a. Figure out the concepts and essential learning objectives of the lesson.
   b. Identify the specific criteria you will evaluate and how you will determine if the criteria have been met well or poorly. Identify four levels of quality, ranging from an excellent response (worth 4 points) to a poor response (worth only 1 point), for each of the criteria to be evaluated.
   c. Write these into the corresponding spaces in the grid you created in Step 3 above.
   d. When you are pleased with the results, transfer your criteria and evaluation standards into the corresponding boxes on the blank template provided on the companion CD.
   e. Give your students a copy of the rubric at the same time they get their assignment so that they will better understand the criteria on which they will be judged.

For more information online, go to:

http://intranet.cps.k12.il.us/Assessments/Ideas_and_Rubrics/Create_Rubric/create_rubric.html

SOURCE: Adapted from curriculum at Palm Middle School, Lemon Grove, CA.

Excel

Excel

CLASS GRADE BOOK

Project Number:	XL-03
Additional hardware:	None
Internet connection required?	No
Template available?	Yes
Grade Level:	Elementary, Middle School, High School

3

Medium Difficulty

Created by:

Teacher

Project type:

Administrative

Student learning style: N/A

Not Applicable

Approximate time: 30 minutes to create a one-semester grade book

Content Area:

Language Arts

Math

Science

Social Studies

Comments: Perhaps no single document is more important to a classroom teacher than the gradebook. Despite this fact, amazingly few teacher preparation courses show teacher candidates how to set one up. The novice teacher must seek guidance from a more experienced mentor on how to best keep track of student performance in the classroom. Using the unique features of automated spreadsheets, Excel can be used to create useful and innovative gradebooks for tracking student performance, showing classroom trends, and creating various charts and graphs to monitor student performance.

Procedures:

1. Open a Microsoft Excel spreadsheet. If you prefer, open the sample spreadsheet shown next and included on the companion CD.

2. Across Row 2, label the tops of columns for Last Name, First Name. Label subsequent columns with class dates. Replace the student names on the sample template with the actual names of your students. The sample template lists only five students. For more students, simply copy and paste the six rows (name, attendance, homework, assignments, quiz, test) as many times as needed for all students.

3. Beginning with the row under the first student's name in Column A, list the criteria that will be used to track student performance. In the sample shown here and on the companion CD, student grades will be based on attendance, homework, assignments, quizzes, and tests.

4. Enter these same criteria (attendance, homework, assignments, etc.) as column headings following the class dates columns.

5. In the example indicated for attendance, mark 1 for present and 0 for absent. The calculation then figures attendance as a percentage based on total days of school. The homework and assignments totals are just the sum of all the individual homework and assignment grades. The quiz and test averages are the mathematical averages of the combined scores in these areas. Determine the scoring criteria to be used for each category and enter the appropriate calculation in the formula box for the appropriate cell. If you wish to use different calculations from those in the sample to figure grades in each area, replace the formula in the appropriate cell with the desired formula. Copy and paste this new cell into the correct position for each student. See Excel Help for more information on designing formulas.

		9/9	9/10	9/11	9/12	9/13	9/16	9/17	9/18	9/19	9/20		Attend %	Homework Total	Assignment Total	Quiz Avg	Test Avg
	Date																
Anderson,	**Andy**																
	Attendance	1	1	1	0	1	0	0	1	1	1		70				
	Homework	10	10	8	10		6	2	10	10				66			
	Assignment	10	20	15	15	15	20	20	20	3	10				148		
	Quiz Scores		15		15			12		10						13	
	Test Scores					98					85						91.5
Boop,	**Betty**																
	Attendance	1	1	1	1	1	1	1		1	1		90				
	Homework	10	5	10	10		10	10	10	10				75			
	Assignment	10	15	16	16	17	12	20	20	19	17				162		
	Quiz Scores		15		15			15		15						15	
	Test Scores					78					89						83.5
Conrad,	**Chris**																
	Attendance	1	0	1	1	1	1	1	0	1	0		70				
	Homework	10	10	10	10		10	10	10	10				80			
	Assignment	15	15	15	15	15	15	15	15	15	15				150		
	Quiz Scores		0		15			15		15						11.25	
	Test Scores					100					100						100
Devonshire,	**Deshonte**																
	Attendance	1	0	0	0	1	1	1	1	1	1		70				
	Homework	0	8	0	5		2	0	4	4				23			
	Assignment	7	7	7	5	8	6	6	5	8	3				62		
	Quiz Scores		0		0			15		15						7.5	
	Test Scores					64					38						51
Edwards,	**Eric**																
	Attendance	1	1	1	1	1	0	1	1	1	1		90				
	Homework	7	6	8	8		6	4	10	10				59			
	Assignment	10	11	8	10	14	11	10	9	8	10				101		

For more information online, go to:

http://www.Internet4classrooms.com/excel_grade.htm

SELF-CHECKING QUIZ

3

Medium Difficulty

Project Number:	XL-04
Additional hardware:	None
Internet connection required?	No
Template available?	Yes
Grade Level:	Elementary, Middle School, High School

Created by:

Teacher

Project type:

Instructional

Student learning style:

Visual

Approximate time: 30 minutes to create a 10-question quiz

Content Area:

Language Arts

Math

Science

Social Studies

Comments: Self-checking quizzes can be used in a variety of ways. They can be used as a preassessment tool to determine what students already know about a topic prior to planning the lesson. This project could also be paricularly useful in helping students review for a test. The sample shown here is available on the accompanying companion CD and can be modified as needed to fit the situation. While this project may seem rather involved initially, once you have created it, it can be easily modified for repeated use.

Procedures:

1. Open a Microsoft Excel worksheet. Add the quiz title.

2. Head Columns B through D with Question, Your Answer, and Response. Head Column E with Correct Answer (after you have entered all the information for this quiz, go back and change all entries in this last column to white font (see Step 8), so the students can't see the answers).

3. Select the column where you want to place the questions and possible answers. Click on the letter at the top of that column to highlight the entire column. On the toolbar, select **Format > Cells**. On the window that appears, select the **Alignment** tab and check the box marked

Wrap text. This will allow you to enter multiple lines of text in a single cell using the word wrap feature. Use this column for the questions and answers as described in the next step.

5. In Cell D5 (or a different cell where you want the response to appear), enter the following formula: =IF(C5=E5,"Way to Go!","OOPS! Try Again").

6. If you prefer to have a different response, replace the words "Way To Go/OOPS! Try Again" with "Right/Wrong" in the preceding formula.

7. Copy and paste the above formula into each cell in Column D that corresponds to one of your questions.

8. The Excel program will determine if the answer the student gives is correct or not by comparing his or her answer in Column C with the desired answer listed in Column E. Enter the letters for the correct answers to your questions in Column E.

9. Click on the top of Column E to highlight the entire column, select **Format > Cells > Font > Color**. Select white on the color palette, then click **OK**. This will help to "hide" the correct answers from the student. If you prefer, you can use any other column to the right of the quiz to store the correct answers. If you chose to use a different column, like Column Z for instance, go back and replace E5 with Z5 in the formula above, then copy the corrected formula in the proper cells.

Self-Checking Quiz

Question	Your Answer	Response
1. Who is buried in Grant's tomb? ___a. Robert E. Lee ___b. Stonewall Jackson ___c. Ulysses S. Grant ___d. Peter Piper	c	Way to Go!
2. When was the Declaration of Independence signed? ___a. July 4, 1776 ___b. July 4, 1976 ___c. December 25, 1607 ___d. March 15, 105 b.c.	a	Way to Go!
3. This is a: ___a. Kar ___b. Care ___c. Kahr ___d. Car	a	OOPS! Try Again
4. The opposite of "Here" is: ___a. Their ___b. There ___c. They're ___d. Thair	b	Way to Go!
5. The Space Shuttle is designed to orbit: ___a. The Earth ___b. The Moon ___c. The Sun ___d. The Planet Krypton	a	Way to Go!

Excel

SKELETAL SYSTEM

3

Medium Difficulty

Project Number: XL-05

Additional hardware: None

Internet connection required? Yes

Template available? Yes

Grade Level: Elementary, Middle School, High School

Created by: Teacher

Project type: Instructional

Student learning style: Visual

Approximate time: 15 minutes to create one diagram for labeling

Content Area: Science

Comments: Many projects involve identifying and labeling component parts of a system. In this example, students will be required to label major bones in the skeletal system. The "Insert Comment" function available with Excel spreadsheets is especially useful for projects like this. The sample project shown here is included on the companion CD.

Excel

Procedures:

1. Find an appropriate image of a skeleton. To do this, search the Internet or electronically scan a picture from some other source. (Be sure your images are free and not copyright protected.) Save this image on your computer. To save an image from the Internet, right-click on the image, select **Save Picture As,** and select a file and file name. In the **Save as Type** box, select **JPEG** from the drop-down menu.

2. Open Microsoft Excel and select **Format > Sheet > Background** and insert the picture you have saved. If the image is too small or too large, go back to the Internet and find another image. This image will be repeated multiple times on the screen. We will deal with that in Step 6.

3. Next, reduce the size of the cells so that the information the student enters will be closest to the actual location on the skeleton. To do this, highlight the entire spreadsheet by clicking on the cell in the extreme upper left corner of the spreadsheet.

4. Select **Format > Column > Width** and set the width to 1.0.

5. Select **Format > Row > Height** and set height to 10.0.

6. This image will be "tiled" repeatedly. To eliminate the duplicate images, highlight a block of the unneeded pictures. Select **Format > Cells > Pattern > Color**. Select a color from the color palette (black works best). This will cover the duplicate images with a solid black background. Repeat the process using different rows and columns until all duplicate images within the screen are covered. Ignore the duplicate images that appear off the screen to the bottom and the right.

7. Next, eliminate the grid lines. Select **Tools > Options > View** and remove the checkmark beside **Gridlines**. Click OK.

8. To enter information on the picture, have the student click on the image where he or she wants the words to appear. Select **Insert > Comment**. Type the comment, name of the bone, or other text in the yellow comment box that appears. Moving the cursor makes the comment box disappear, leaving a small red triangle in its place.

9. Pass the cursor over this mark and the comment box reappears, revealing any information stored there.

10. To change a comment once it has been added, right click on the red triangle and select **Edit Comment** or **Delete Comment**.

11. The final skeleton may look something like the image shown here.

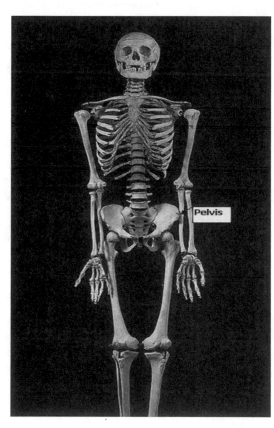

FIVE IN A ROW

Project Number:	XL-06
Additional hardware:	None
Internet connection required?	No
Template available?	Yes
Grade Level:	Elementary, Middle School, High School

Medium Difficulty

Created by:

Teacher

Project type:

Instructional

Student learning style:

Visual

Approximate time: 30 minutes to create one game board

Content Area:

Language Arts   Math   Science   Social Studies

Comments: Five in a Row is a fun game that can be played by as few as two or three individuals or as many as five or six teams for full class participation. This can be used to review previously studied material or as a fun means of assessing student knowledge prior to instructing a unit. In addition to the content being addressed, it will also help refine student comprehension of grid coordinate systems. This game board can be used in a variety of ways. One possible set of rules follows, but feel free to make up your own rules as you see fit.

Procedures:

1. Open Project XL-13, Five in a Row on the companion CD included with this book.

2. Assign a color to each player or team. Have the first player identify a grid square that he or she would like to claim with a color. The teacher then asks the player a question. If the player answers correctly, the teacher will color the cell the player's color. If the player answers incorrectly, play moves to the next player in turn.

3. To color a grid square, select the desired square, then click **Format > Cells > Patterns** tab. Click on the desired color and exit the menu. The cell will then become the selected color.

4. The game ends when a player colors five squares in a line. Lines may run horizontally, vertically, or diagonally.

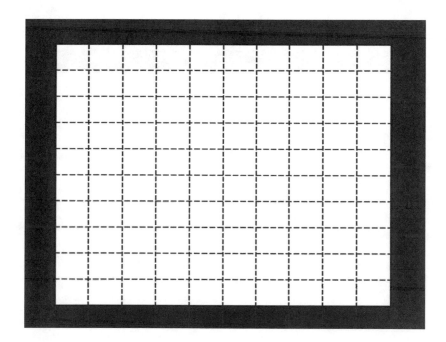

5. Each cell answered correctly is worth 1 point, except for select grid squares that have 2 or 3 points. These special cells will show their added point value when given any color except white. The locations of the bonus squares are illustrated next. The first player to get Five in a Row earns an additional 10 bonus points.

6. Add up the points to determine the winner.

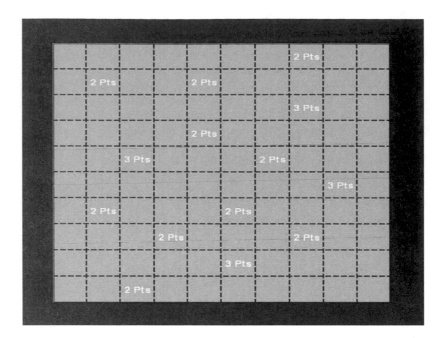

7. Players may try to block an opponent's run, by selecting cells in line with those already colored.

8. If you prefer, you can create your own Five in a Row grid from scratch. To do this, open an Excel spreadsheet and shade the cells in a 10 x 10 grid. Adjust cell width and cell height as needed to make the cells square in shape.

9. Randomly select cells around the board and enter 2 Pts or 3 Pts. Color the font of these numbers white so they can't be seen until that cell is selected.

ANNOTATED FAMILY TREE

3

Medium Difficulty

Project Number: XL-07

Additional hardware: Scanner

Internet connection required? No

Template available? Yes

Grade Level: Elementary, Middle School, High School

Created by:

Student

Project type:

Instructional

Student learning style:

Visual

Approximate time: 45 minutes to create a five-generation, annotated family tree

Content Area:

Language Arts

Science

Comments: One of the favored activities during family gatherings is the retelling of stories that have become part of the family lore. Many students, as they begin to develop a sense of self-identity, are interested in knowing more about their ancestors. Whether they came to town on the Mayflower, on a covered wagon, or in a station wagon, this sense of identity can be reinforced with an understanding of one's personal heritage. The Annotated Family Tree is a useful tool in developing students' self-esteem and a sense of belonging to something bigger than they are. Additionally, one of the first steps to becoming a more culturally responsive student is to first have an understanding of one's own culture. This Annotated Family Tree can help.

Procedures:

1. Open a new Excel spreadsheet. Place the cursor on the top, lettered row of cells. By clicking and dragging the dividing line between columns to the left or right, you can adjust the width of the column. Increase the width of Columns A through E until they each can comfortably hold about 20 characters on a single line of text.

2. Next, eliminate the grid lines. Select **Tools > Options > View** and remove the checkmark beside Gridlines. Click **OK.**

3. In Cell C1, enter the name of the family represented by the tree.

4. In Row 2, enter the words Great-Great-Grandparents, Great-Grandparents, Grandparents, and Parents in Cells A2, B2, C2, and D2, respectively.

5. Now to add the branches of the "tree": To select more than one cell, hold the Control (Ctrl) key down while you click on the desired cells. In this manner, highlight the *even* cells A4, A6, A8 and so on, through to cell A34.

6. To mark the proper cells into which you will insert the individual names, you could color the cells with male relatives blue and cells with female relatives pink. To do this, hold the Control button down while clicking on the following cells: A4, A8, A12, A16, A20, A24, A28, B5, B13, B21, B29, C7, C27, and D11. Release the Control button, and select **Format > Cells > Patterns**; then select a light blue color from the color palette, and select **OK**. You have now colored all the cells where you will list the male relatives. For placement of the female relatives, repeat the process for cells A6, A10, A14, A18, A22, A26, A30, A34, B9, B17, B25, B33, C15, C32, and D27. Color these cells pink.

7. Now to draw the horizontal branches of the tree: While holding down the Control key, select each of the colored cells. With these cells selected, go to **Format > Cells > Border**. Next, click on the button that shows the cell with only the bottom line drawn.

8. To draw the vertical lines of the tree branches, select the appropriate cells, go to **Format > Cells > Border**, and select the desired cell border(s) for the cells selected.

9. Enter the names of relatives on the appropriate lines.

10. Now to make the tree interactive: Right click on a cell containing a relative's name. Select **Insert Comment**. A text box will appear. Enter any additional information in this text box, like nickname, place of birth, dates of birth and death, and any other information of interest or claim to fame.

11. When you have finished entering the desired information, click out of the text box. A small red triangle will appear in the upper right corner of the cell. When you place your cursor over the triangle, the text box opens and you can read the information entered previously.

12. For added effect, enter photos of the individuals named on the branches of the tree. To do this, select **Insert** from the drop-down menu, then **Picture > From File.** Navigate to the desired file where the pictures are stored, select the desired picture, and adjust size and location as needed.

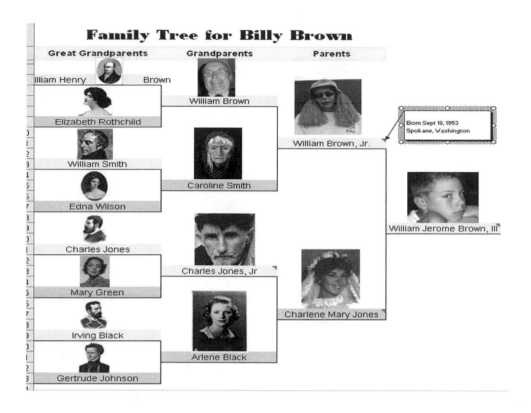

For more information online, go to:

http://office.microsoft.com/en-au/templates/TC011031501033.aspx

MEASURES OF CENTRAL TENDENCY

3
Medium Difficulty

Project Number:	XL-08
Additional hardware:	None
Internet connection required?	No
Template available?	Yes
Grade Level:	Elementary, Middle School, High School

Created by:
Student and/or Teacher

Project type:
Instructional

Student learning style:
Visual

Approximate time: 30 minutes to create one interactive data collection table

Content Area:
Math

Comments: One of the fundamental math skills students are taught deals with measures of central tendency. The ability to calculate mean, median, and mode of a set of numbers is important as they develop number sense. Using Microsoft Excel, you can create a spreadsheet that will make these calculations automatically. This project will allow you to reinforce the math concepts as they are taught. Project XL-08 on the accompanying CD has a template ready for immediate use in the classroom.

Procedures:

1. Open Project XL-08 on the accompanying companion CD.

2. This project will allow you to compute the sum, mean, median, and mode for a group of objects sharing some criteria. Additionally, it will identify the minimum and maximum values in the set and determine the range within which all values fall. This particular project is designed to allow you to determine the measures of central tendency for various colored pieces in several packs of M&M's ® candies, but it can be modified accordingly to support other tasks.

3. Have children sort and count the colors of candies in several packages of candy. Enter the values in the upper left quadrant of the XL-08 spreadsheet.

4. The measures of central tendency by color will appear in the upper right quadrant. Similar measures by package will appear in the lower left quadrant. A graph of all values is displayed in the lower right quadrant.

5. If you prefer to design your own project, determine how many rows and columns you want in your grid. This is where you will enter your data.

6. Determine in which cells you want to display your measures of central tendency. Select the desired cell, and enter the required formula on the formula line. In the following formulas, put the beginning and ending cells of the rows or columns that hold the data you want to manipulate. List these two cells within the parentheses in the formulas, separated by a colon.

7. The formulas are as follows:
   To find the sum, enter = SUM(C4:G4)
   To find mean, enter = AVERAGE(C4:G4)
   To find median, enter = MEDIAN(C4:G4)
   To find mode, enter = MODE(C4:G4)
   To find minimum value, = MIN(C4:G4)
   To find maximum value, = MAX(C4:G4)
   To find range of values, = N4-M4

8. Color the rows or columns as desired to make the data grid easier to read.

Excel

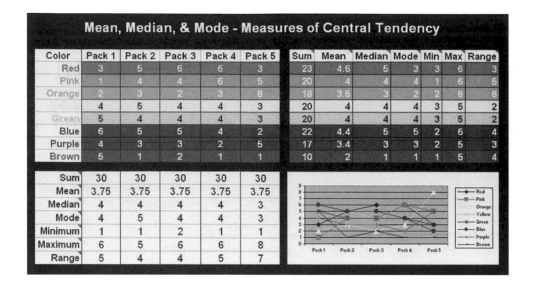

For more information online, go to:

http://ctap295.borderlink.org/cdenton/index.html

Thanks to Lisa E. Heaton for creating an earlier version of this project.

RATIOS, FRACTIONS, DECIMALS, PERCENTAGES

3

Medium Difficulty

Project Number: XL-09

Additional hardware: None

Internet connection required? No

Template available? Yes

Grade Level: Elementary, Middle School, High School

Created by:

Teacher

Project type:

Instructional

Student learning style:

Visual

Approximate time: 30 minutes to create a conversion data table

Content Area:

Math

Comments: Some of the more challenging topics to teach in elementary math classes are the concepts of ratio, fractions, decimals, and percentages. One approach to this task is to help students recognize equivalency between these functions. Using the Excel spreadsheet for this project on the companion CD, you can present each of these concepts in visual format to your students.

Procedures:

1. Open Project XL-09 on the companion CD included with this text.

2. Insert different values in the white boxes in the ratio section of the spreadsheet. The Excel math functions will automatically calculate and post the values for the equivalent fraction, decimal, and percentages indicated by the ratio values.

3. Additionally, the pie chart will provide a visual display of the information. NOTE: The pie chart will work properly only for fractional values less than 1 (i.e., the numerator is less than the denominator).

4. To use this project in class: You could have the students estimate the fraction, decimal, and percentages values for given ratios, then plug the values into the spreadsheet and check the accuracy of their estimate.

5. If you prefer to create your own number converter, open an Excel worksheet and determine in which cells you want to enter the values of the ratio. For example, enter the first value of the ratio in cell C5, and the second number of the ratio in cell E5.

6. Decide where you want to display the fraction, decimal, and percentage equivalents.

7. Select the cells where the answer is to be displayed and enter the following formulas on the formula line:

Fraction numerator	This is the cell where the first number in the ratio is displayed. In the example cited here, select cell I5. On the formula bar for this cell, enter "=C5" (without the quotation marks).
Fraction denominator	This is the cell where the second number in the ratio is displayed. In the example cited here, select cell I6. On the formula bar for this cell, enter "=E5" (without the quotation marks).
Decimal value	This is the cell where you will display the decimal value of the ratio. In the example cited here, select cell M5. On the formula bar for this cell, enter = (numerator cell/denominator cell). In this example, the formula will read "=C5/E5" (without the quotation marks).
Percentage	This is the cell where you will display the percentage value of the ratio. In the example cited here, select cell Q5. On the formula bar for this cell, enter =(numerator cell/denominator cell). In this example, the formula will read "=C5/E5" (without the quotation marks).

8. To express the quotient in the desired style, select **Format > Cells > Number**, then select **Number, Percentage**, or **Fraction** as desired. Select the cell where the answer is to be displayed.

9. Select **Format > Cells > Number**, then select **Number, Percentage**, or **Fraction** as desired.

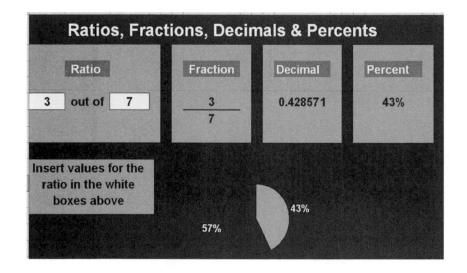

For more information online, go to:

http://www.mathgoodies.com/lessons/vol4/fractions_to_percents.html

Thanks to Lisa E. Heaton for an earlier version of this project.

Excel

Excel

COUNTING COINS

Project Number:	XL-10
Additional hardware:	None
Internet connection required?	Yes
Template available?	Yes
Grade Level:	Elementary, Middle School

4
Difficult

Created by:

Teacher

Project type:

Instructional

Student learning style:

Visual

Approximate time: 45 minutes to create a six-coin conversion spreadsheet

Content Area:

Language Arts

Comments: A basic skill taught in the lower elementary grades is the ability to count coins and recognize their value. Additionally, children who understand coin values may have an easier time learning to manipulate those values when adding or subtracting money. The child who understands that 10 pennies make a dime and that 10 dimes make a dollar is better prepared to transfer that learning to the concept of regrouping and place value in basic math algorithms. Using the math functions available in Excel, you can create an interactive spreadsheet to help your students master these concepts. This project may be best suited for students who need a calculator to check their work that they may have already done on a different, teacher-provided worksheet.

Procedures:

1. A completed spreadsheet has been created for your use. Open Project XL-10 on the accompanying companion CD.

2. This sheet is designed to automatically perform the required additions, allowing the student to check the work and get immediate feedback on answers.

3. In Column E on the accompanying spreadsheet, enter a desired number of coins of each denomination. When you press Tab, Enter, or an arrow key to move off the selected cell, the Excel math function will automatically compute the value in cents, nickels, dimes, quarters, half-dollars, and dollars.

4. The total amount of the coinage selected will appear in the lower right corner of the spreadsheet.

5. If you are not working with the higher denomination coins, simply enter 0 for their value in Column E.

6. If you wish to create your own Coin Counting project, open a new Excel spreadsheet.

7. Insert images of the various denominations of coins in a vertical column down the left side of the spreadsheet.

8. Along the top row, head columns for Cents, Nickels, Dimes, Quarters, Half-Dollars, and Dollars.

9. Identify the cell where you want the student to enter the numbers of the different coins being considered.

10. Identify and select the cells where you want the answer displayed.

11. With the designated cell selected, enter the conversion formula on the formula line. Be certain the formula contains the cell identifier where the original number of coins to be converted is located.

Excel

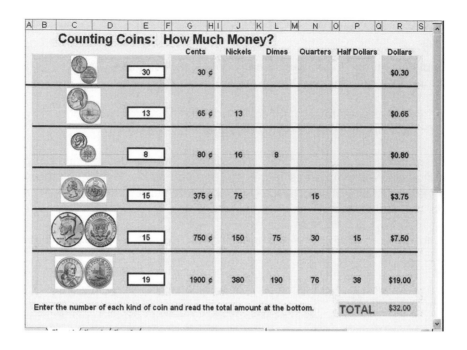

			Cents	Nickels	Dimes	Quarters	Half Dollars	Dollars
		30	30 ¢					$0.30
		13	65 ¢	13				$0.65
		8	80 ¢	16	8			$0.80
		15	375 ¢	75		15		$3.75
		15	750 ¢	150	75	30	15	$7.50
		19	1900 ¢	380	190	76	38	$19.00

Enter the number of each kind of coin and read the total amount at the bottom.   **TOTAL** $32.00

For more information online, go to:

http://www.coe.uh.edu/archive/math/math_lessons/mathles5.html

Excel

MATH FOUR-FUNCTION WORKSHEETS

4
Difficult

Project Number: XL-11

Additional hardware: None

Internet connection required? No

Template available? Yes

Grade Level: Elementary, Middle School, High School

Created by:
Teacher

Project type:
Instructional

Student learning style:
Visual

Approximate time: 10 minutes to create a 20-question worksheet

Content Area:
Math

Comments: Excel has some wonderful classroom applications. Using the powerful math functions within this program, you can create all manner of worksheets to practice newly learned skills or to assess skill mastery of information taught previously. This project will allow you to create a self-grading worksheet that will allow students to practice the desired math function (add, subtract, multiply, or divide).

Excel

Procedures:

1. Open a new Excel spreadsheet.

2. Type in a math problem placing only a single element of the problem per cell in a row. For example, in the problem 3 + 5 = _, you should place the 3, the +, the 5, and the = in each of four consecutive cells along a row. Leave the fifth cell blank for the student to record the answer.

3. Click on the sixth cell in the same row. Here you will enter the formula that will be used for all addition problems. Formulas always start with an equal sign "=", followed immediately by the next character with no space following.

4. For addition problems, on the formula line, type in the following statement: =IF(ISBLANK (F3),"",IF(F3=($B3+D3),"Good","Not Quite")).

5. For this particular problem, when the student places an answer in the fifth cell, the words "Good" or "Not Quite" will appear in the sixth cell, depending on whether the answer given was right or wrong.

6. Continue inserting problems using the same math function in a verticle column.

7. Once you have entered all your addition problems in horizontal format, select the cell where you first entered the addition formula. Notice there is a small + sign in the lower right corner of the cell. To copy the formula so it works for all the problems in the column, place your cursor over the lower right corner of the cell. Click and drag the cell down to the bottom of the column.

8. The key to making this work is in entering the correct equation in the function box at the end of each problem. The equations to be entered are as follows:
For addition: =IF(ISBLANK(F15),"",IF(F15=($B15+D15),"Good","Not Quite"))
For subtraction: =IF(ISBLANK(M3),"",IF(M3=($I3-K3),"Super!!!","Oops"))
For multiplication: =IF(ISBLANK(T3),"",IF(T3=($P3*R3),"Yep","Nope"))
For division: =IF(ISBLANK(AA3),"",IF(AA3=($W3/Y3),"Correct","Incorrect"))

9. Once you have entered the formula in Cell 6, highlight that cell. Click on the lower right corner of that cell and drag it down the column for as many rows as you plan to have problems using that particular function.

10. If you want to add problems using a different function, go across the spreadsheet to the ninth column and repeat the process, being certain you adjust the function equation to properly reflect the actual cells in use.

11. A sample template has been included on the companion CD. Download the project to your computer and change the numerical values of the equations as desired, making certain to remain function-consistent down any given column.

Addition Practice Page					Subtraction Practice Page					Multiplication Practice Page					Division Practice Page				
8	+	2	=		6	-	7	=		3	x	5	=		6	/	2	=	
4	+	9	=		27	-	16	=		4	x	6	=		20	/	-5	=	
-2	+	-4	=		20	-	10	=		2	x	3	=		16	/	4	=	
3	+	-5	=		37	-	17	=		5	x	9	=		9	/	-3	=	
6	+	-6	=		-24	-	12	=		6	x	4	=		24	/	8	=	
-1	+	9	=		200	-	150	=		6	x	8	=		60	/	12	=	
-3	+	7	=		45	-	15	=		3	x	6	=		36	/	12	=	
4	+	-6	=		29	-	-40	=		8	x	5	=		12	/	-3	=	
-4	+	-4	=		36	-	30	=		10	x	2	=		18	/	3	=	
-3	+	9	=		-3	-	16	=		2	x	1	=		4	/	2	=	
7	+	-2	=		24	-	12	=		5	x	5	=		18	/	-6	=	
9	+	9	=		-5	-	3	=		9	x	3	=		25	/	-5	=	
8	+	-9	=		50	-	-25	=		2	x	8	=		45	/	3	=	
7	+	9	=		18	-	30	=		4	x	5	=		27	/	3	=	
-7	+	10	=		-9	-	-11	=		5	x	7	=		18	/	-9	=	

For more information online, go to:

http://www.usd.edu/trio/tut/excel/

Thanks to Lisa E. Heaton for this idea.

Excel

Excel

INTERACTIVE MAP

Difficult

Project Number: XL-12

Additional hardware: None

Internet connection required? No

Template available? Yes

Grade Level: Elementary, Middle School, High School

Created by:
Student and/or Teacher

Project type:
Instructional

Student learning style:
Visual

Approximate time: 20 minutes to create one map for editing

Content Area:
Social Studies

Science

Comments: Many students, especially younger students, are fascinated by maps. Whether "treasure maps" showing the location of hidden riches or a city map from the local gas station, maps can be used to spark interest in the geography of a given area. And what student isn't interested, at least in passing, to see where his or her home, town, state, or nation is in relation to others? Map-reading skills are an important component in state-mandated curriculum standards. This project might be perfectly suited for group work, where several children are responsible for researching information on designated states, then pooling their information into a composite map of the entire nation. As a related project, see PP-15, Where I Live.

Procedures:

1. Locate a digitized map of the desired area. A map of the United States is included on the sample provided on the companion CD, but you can use any digitized map for this project, providing the size of the image is around 400 pixels by 600 pixels. Much smaller and the image may lack the needed detail, and much larger, all of the image may not be visible on screen at one time. Save the map on your computer.

2. Open Microsoft Excel and select **Format > Sheet > Background** and insert the map picture you have saved. If the image is too small or too large, go back to the Internet and find another image.

3. Next, reduce the size of the cells so that the information the student enters will be closest to the actual location on the map. To do this, highlight the entire spreadsheet by clicking on the cell in the extreme upper left corner of the spreadsheet. This will highlight the entire sheet. Select **Format > Column > Width** and set the width to 1.0. Next, select **Format > Row > Height** and select 10.

4. This image will be "tiled" repeatedly. To eliminate the duplicate images, highlight a series of rows immediately below the desired portion of the image. Select **Format > Cells > Pattern > Color**. Select a color from the color palette (black works best). This will cover the duplicate images with a solid black background. Repeat the process using different rows and columns until all duplicate images within the screen are covered.

5. Next, eliminate the grid lines. Select **Tools > Options > View** and remove the checkmark beside **Gridlines**. Click **OK**.

6. To enter information on the picture, have the student click on the image where he or she wants the words to appear. In the sample map provided on the companion CD, click on the desired state. Select **Insert > Comment**. Type the comment (state slogan, capital city, population, industry, etc.) in the comment box that appears. Moving the cursor makes the comment box disappear, leaving a small red triangle in its place. Pass the cursor over this mark and the comment box reappears.

7. To change a comment once it has been added, right click on the red triangle and select **Edit Comment** or **Delete Comment**.

8. The final map may look something like the example below. On the sample Interactive Map on the companion CD, move the cursor over the small red triangles in Texas, Alaska, Hawaii, or Montana for the information boxes to pop up.

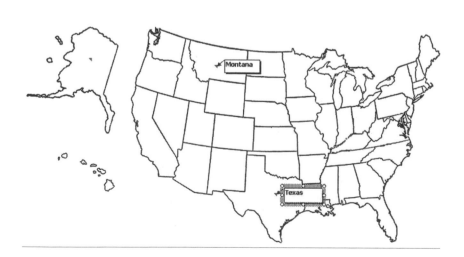

PRACTICE WITH MULTIPLICATION

5

Very Difficult

Project Number: XL-13

Additional hardware: None

Internet connection required? No

Template available? Yes

Grade Level: Elementary, Middle School, High School

Created by:

Teacher

Project type:

Instructional

Student learning style:

Visual

Approximate time: 60 minutes to create an eight-problem worksheet

Content Area:

2
+3
5

Math

Comments: For students struggling with learning multiplication, it can be a challenge getting them to practice the skills necessary to master the multiplication algorithm. Using Microsoft Excel, you can create a spreadsheet where your students can practice these skills, answering math problems and receiving immediate feedback. While the steps needed to generate a multiplication spreadsheet from scratch can prove cumbersome, such a project has been created and included as Project XL-13 on the companion CD included with this book.

Procedures:

1. Open Project XL-13 on the companion CD.

2. This sheet is designed with sample problems and empty cells where students can enter their answers.

3. To the right of each problem is a collection of cells corresponding to the empty cells in the problem. As students enter their answers, the corresponding cell will indicate a checkmark for correct responses and an X mark for incorrect responses.

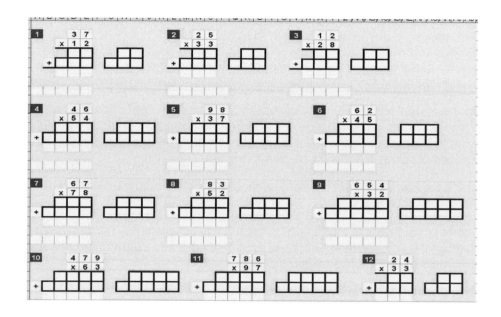

4. When the entire problem has been completed, words will appear underneath the problem indicating whether the response is correct or incorrect.

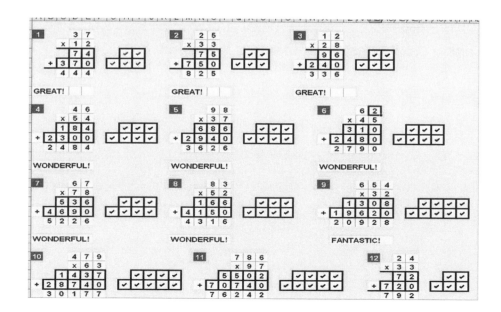

5. This is one of the more challenging projects to create from scratch. Because of this, you may want to limit your input to just changing the values of the factors and the product rather than starting an entire worksheet from scratch.

6. You may want to create your own multiplication problems based on the existing projects on the companion CD. To do this, select math problems from the template that have the same number of place holders, in the same positions, as the problem you wish to use. On a separate sheet of paper, work out your desired problem, displaying the correct digits as they will appear in the finished project.

7. Carefully record the original answers to each of the math problems on a sheet of paper. Save these answers for later use in Step 13 below.

8. Replace the digits in the existing multiplication problems on the spreadsheet with those of your choosing that you worked out in Step 6.

9. For each place holder in the set of blocks to the right of the problems, you will need to adjust the corresponding formula to mirror that in the revised multiplication problem.

10. Click on an individual cell in the collection of cells to the right of the problems. The formula will appear in the formula block at the top of the spreadsheet. In this formula, replace the digit in the final set of parentheses with the new digit in the corresponding block in the multiplication problem. Do this for all cells in the set.

11. If you have done this step correctly, a checkmark should appear in each of the cells to the right of the problems.

12. To be sure the words at the bottom of the problem acknowledge correct answers, place your cursor on the first cell in the series of comment cells and note the formula that appears on the formula line at the top of the spreadsheet.

13. In this formula, find the digits that immediately follow the = sign. Carefully replace each of the digits from the original answer (recorded in Step 7) with the correct digits from the new answer (recorded in Step 6 above). Each digit may be replaced several times, depending on the length of the answer and the place value of the digit. If you have done this step accurately, an affirming comment should appear in the row of cells below the problem.

For more information online, go to:

http://www.multiplication.com

Thanks to Tammy Davis for an earlier version of this project.

Excel

5

Microsoft Access Projects

In this chapter you will find the following activities:

Project Number	Title	Difficulty	Created By
AC-01	Reading List	2	Student and/or Teacher
AC-02	U.S. Presidents	2	Student
AC-03	Exercise Program	2	Student and/or Teacher
AC-04	United States of America	2	Student and/or Teacher
AC-05	Weather Observations	2	Student
AC-06	The Continents	2	Student
AC-07	Planets	2	Student
AC-08	Class Library	2	Student and/or Teacher
AC-09	Geometric Shapes	3	Student and/or Teacher
AC-10	Video List	3	Teacher
AC-11	Student Data	3	Teacher
AC-12	Clouds	3	Student
AC-13	Student Behavior	3	Student and/or Teacher
AC-14	Peer Review	4	Student and/or Teacher

Access

INTRODUCTION TO MICROSOFT ACCESS

Of the programs available in the Microsoft Office suite, perhaps Microsoft Access is the least understood and used. But properly employed, this little gem can revolutionize the way you keep records in your classroom. Microsoft Access is a relational database program. Access allows you to create a database on almost any topic of your choosing. You can add, delete, sort, and display data in a database. You can create forms to enter data into the database, then select data of interest using the query function, and finally, display these data using the report function. A relational database is one that allows Access to link to tables that have similar fields. In this way, you can modify information in one database, such as a list of items or students in a drop-down menu, and have it appear when you click on that field on another designated form.

Access databases are perfect for keeping track of a myriad of things in the classroom. Often, they are used for phone, mailing, or contact lists, but they have many other uses as well. Instead of a card catalog, create an Access database to catalog the videos in a collection or the books in your class library. For science, you may want to create a database of the characteristics of the planets in the solar system or monitor and track the weather. In language arts, use Access to record and track required reading lists. For social studies, you may want to use it to record facts about the 50 United States.

Although the mechanics of creating an Access form and linking it to a table may seem somewhat involved, there are 14 Access projects on the accompanying companion CD that are already created and just waiting for you or your students to enter the data. Go on. Give it a try. You'll wonder how you ever got along so well for so long without it.

Access

READING LIST

2

Easy

Project Number:	AC-01
Additional hardware:	None
Internet connection required?	No
Template available?	Yes
Grade Level:	Elementary, Middle School, High School

Created by:

Student and/or
Teacher

Project type:

Administrative

Student learning style:

N/A
Not Applicable

Approximate time: 15 minutes to create a 10-book data table

Content Area:

Language Arts

Comments: Early development of reading skills is crucial to student success. Classrooms arranged to present a language-rich environment are becoming the norm in schoolhouses today. Students should be encouraged to read long, often, and across the curriculum. You may wish to design a program that encourages your students to read. Students could be rewarded based on a predetermined number of reading points earned. Microsoft Access can be used to design a database for tracking the number of reading points earned by your students. The database used in this example is similar to that designed for documenting a class library, but it requires fewer entries and provides an additional space for documenting points earned for reading the indicated books.

Access

Procedures:

1. From the companion CD, open Microsoft Access Project AC-01, Reading List.

2. From the left-hand column, select **Forms**.

3. Open the Reading List Form. This will give you a form for entering information about each of the books your students read.

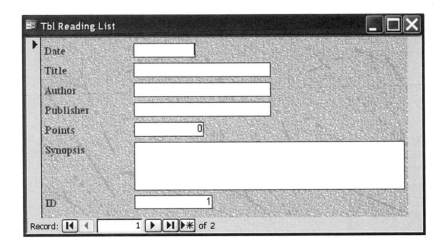

4. Enter data on the form, including date, book title, author, publisher, number of points awarded, and a brief synopsis of the book.

5. To see the information in table format, minimize the Reading List Form and select **Tables** from the left-hand column.

6. Select **Reading List Table.** Here you will see the data you entered for all your books in a single table.

7. If you would prefer to develop your own database, see the following section—"Designing an Access Database."

Date	Title	Author	Publisher	Points	Synopsis	ID
				0		1
				0		2
				0		(AutoNumber)

Reading List Table : Table

Designing an Access Database

You may wish to create your own Access database rather than use one of the provided templates. Although designing your own Access Project may be involved, it is not terribly difficult once you become familiar with the process.

1. There are four basic parts to an Access database, and we will briefly review each of these in turn: tables, forms, queries, and reports. The table is the basis for all other components. This is where the data will reside, and it will define the basic structure of your project.

2. Open Microsoft Access.

3. Select **New > Blank Database**. Give your new database a name and file location.

Tables

1. Select **Create Table in Design View**. Here you will enter the field names you want for your database. Here you identify the specific data elements you want to record. Let us suppose we want to maintain a database of the fish in the classroom fish tank. We might have field names for fish type, length, scale color, sex, weight, and name. Use the **Field Property** box to modify the properties of the fields if the default criteria need to be changed.

2. Select **Save As** and name the table. If asked to define a primary key, select **yes.**

3. Select **View > Datasheet View**. Here you will see the table you have created, and you can add data directly into this table if you wish. If you want to make changes to the table layout, return to **Design View** to do so.

Forms

1. Rather than enter the data directly into the table, another way to enter information into the database is through a form. Forms have spaces to fill in that contain specific information.

2. You can add or remove fields from your form after your create it if you want. On opening the database, select **Forms > Create form by using wizard** from the menu on the left side of the window.

3. The **Available Fields** window will list all the fields you created when you designed the table above. Select the fields you want to appear on your form and move them to the **Selected Fields** box on your screen. Choose the desired layout, style, and form title as directed by the form wizard. Select **Finish.**

4. When you enter data into this newly created form, it will automatically update your table.

Queries

1. To pull selected information out of your database, you can create a query. In the example above, you may want a list of the names of all the fish in the classroom fish tank.

2. Select **Queries > Create query by using wizard**. From the **Available Fields** box, identify which ones you want in your query and move these to the **Selected Fields** box. Select **Next** and give your query a name and select **Finish.** You will now have a table containing only the fields of interest.

Reports

1. Finally, you can generate reports from your Access database. Open the database and select **Reports > Create report by using wizard**.

2. Here again, move the desired information fields from the **Available Fields** box to the **Selected Fields** box. Select **Next.**

3. Select any desired grouping levels, sort order, report layout, style, and report title as directed by the report wizard.

4. When you are satisfied with the overall layout, print your report.

For more information online, go to:

http://www.ed.gov/about/offices/list/ovae/pi/hsinit/papers/reader.doc

http://office.microsoft.com/en-us/access/FX100646921033.aspx

http://www.brainbell.com/tutorials/ms-office/Access_2003/

Access

U.S. Presidents

Project Number: AC-02

Additional hardware: None

Internet connection required? No

Template available? Yes

Grade Level: Elementary, Middle School, High School

2
Easy

Created by:
Student

Project type:
Instructional

Student learning style:
Visual

Approximate time: 30 minutes to create a 10-president factsheet

Content Area:
Social Studies

Comments: Almost every school-age child in America spends some time studying U.S. presidents. Throughout the study of American history, U.S. presidents and their policies and administrations have played crucial roles. Using the Access database developed for this project, you can have a convenient and interactive way for your students to record what they learn about these world leaders. You may want to have students research different presidents and combine their information into a common database.

Access

Procedures:

1. From the companion CD, open Microsoft Access Project AC-02, U.S. Presidents.

2. From the left-hand column, select **Forms**.

3. Open the Presidents Form. This will give you a form for entering information about each of the U.S. presidents.

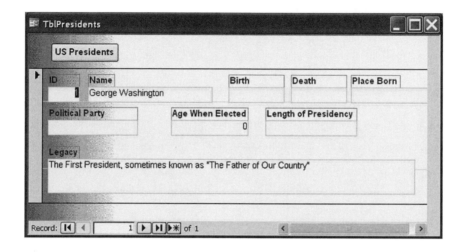

4. Enter data on the form, including a president's name, date of birth, date of death, location of birth, political party affiliation, age at election, length of presidency, and any additional comments. The entry for George Washington has been partially completed by way of example.

5. To see the information in table format, minimize the Presidents Form and select **Tables** from the left-hand column.

6. Select **Presidents Table.** Here you will see the data you entered for all your presidents in a single table.

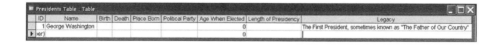

7. Additionally, the form has a command button placed near the top. Return to the **Forms** view and click on the button labeled **Presidents Form**. This button is linked to the Reports function of Access. This will create a summary report showing the name and legacy of each of the presidents entered into the database.

8. If you would prefer to develop your own database, see the "Designing an Access Database" section in Project AC-01.

United States Presidents

ID	Name	Legacy
1	George Washington	The First President came to be known as "The Father of Our Country."
2	Thomas Jefferson	Our Third President drafted the United States Constitution.

For more information online, go to:

http://www.whitehouse.gov/history/presidents/

NOTES

EXERCISE PROGRAM

2

Easy

Project Number:	AC-03
Additional hardware:	None
Internet connection required?	No
Template available?	Yes
Grade Level:	Middle School, High School

Created by:

Student and/or
Teacher

Project type:

Instructional

Student learning style:

Kinesthetic

Approximate time: 5 minutes to document a single exercise session

Content Area:

Math

Comments: Proper physical health is a key element of proper mental health. Exercise, in addition to its many benefits to the body, can serve as an antidote to daily classroom stress. The positive reinforcement of seeing progress over time can serve to encourage individuals who might otherwise give up. The Exercise Program tracker can be used by teacher and student alike. Data recorded over time can be analyzed to determine averages, maximum and minimum values, and other measures of central tendency.

Access

Procedures:

1. From the companion CD, open Microsoft Access Project AC-03, Exercise Program.

2. From the left-hand column, select **Forms.**

3. Open the Exercise Form. This will give you a form for entering information about the exercises done during a workout session.

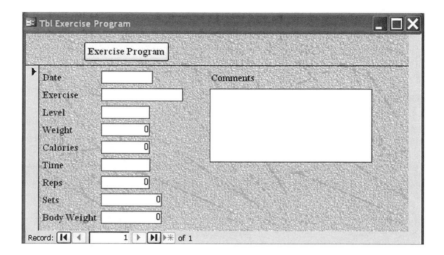

4. There are blank spaces for Date, Exercise Name, Exercise Level, Weight Lifted, Calories Consumed, Duration of Exercise, Number or Repetitions per Set, Number of Sets, Body Weight, and General Comments.

5. To see the information in table format, minimize the Exercise Program Form and select **Tables** from the left-hand column.

6. Select **Exercise Program Table.** Here you will see the data you entered for all your exercise sessions in a single table. By noting changes in the values entered day by day, you can track your progress toward your physical fitness goals.

7. Additionally, the form has a command button placed near the top. Return to the **Forms** view and click on the button labeled **Exercise Program**. This button is linked to the Reports function of Access. This will create a summary report showing the data from each exercise session entered into the database.

8. If you would prefer to develop your own database, see the "Designing an Access Database" section in Project AC-01.

For more information online, go to:

http://www.mayoclinic.com/health/fitness/HQ00171

UNITED STATES OF AMERICA

2
Easy

Project Number: AC-04

Additional hardware: None

Internet connection required? Yes

Template available? Yes

Grade Level: Elementary, Middle School, High School

Created by:
Student and/or
Teacher

Project type:
Instructional

Student learning style:
Visual

Approximate time: 30 minutes to create a 10-state table

Content Area:
Social Studies

Comments: Curriculum requirements in U.S. schools often require that students research details on the various states. Microsoft Access can be used to create a database to store all manner of information about the states in an easily used format. Students can research information on the states, either alone or in groups, enter their data on a Microsoft Access form specially prepared for this purpose, and then read their collected works in a table format. Note: This project may be done in place of, or in conjunction with, Excel Project XL-06, Interactive Map.

Access

Procedures:

1. From the companion CD, open Microsoft Access Project AC-04, The United States of America.

2. From the left-hand column, select **Forms**.

3. Open the U.S. States Form. This will give you a form for entering information about each of the 50 United States.

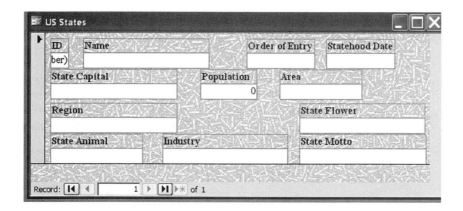

4. Enter data on the form, including the state name, order of entry into the Union, date statehood granted, population, area, region of the country where located, state flower, state animal, primary industries, and state motto.

5. To see the information in table format, minimize the U.S. States Form and select **Tables** from the left-hand column.

6. Select **U.S. States Table.** Here you will see the information you entered for the various states in one table. By selecting **Records > Filter > Advanced Filter Sort**, you can realign your data table in other ways that might make it easier to work with the data. For instance, you may want to sort states alphabetically, by order of entry into the union, by size, or by population.

7. If you would prefer to develop your own database, see the "Designing an Access Database" section in Project AC-01.

For more information online, go to:

http://www.50states.com/

WEATHER OBSERVATIONS

2
Easy

Project Number:	AC-05
Additional hardware:	None
Internet connection required?	Yes
Template available?	Yes
Grade Level:	Elementary, Middle School, High School

Created by:
Student

Project type:
Instructional

Student learning style:
Visual

Aural

Kinesthetic

Approximate time: 10 minutes to create a single day observation

Content Area:
Science

Comments: Students are taught very early on the importance of observation. Like other skills, the power of observation is developed through practice. Daily weather observations can be used to exercise the higher-order thinking skills of cause and effect. Most science curriculums include a study of the weather, and Microsoft Access can be used to record these observations on a daily basis. For related projects, see PP-09, Weather Report; XL-01, Recording Weather; or AC-12, Clouds.

Access

Procedures:

1. From the companion CD, open Microsoft Access Project AC-05, Weather Observations.

2. From the left-hand column, select **Forms**.

3. Open the Weather Observations Form. This will give you a form for entering data based on daily weather conditions.

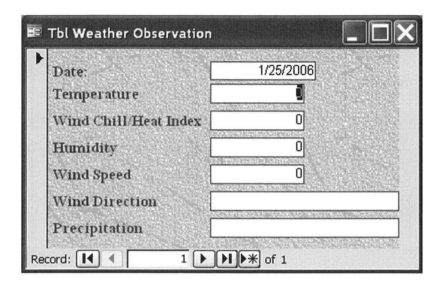

4. Enter data on the form, including date, temperature, wind chill/heat index, humidity, wind speed and direction, and precipitation.

5. To see the information in table format, minimize the Weather Observation Form and select **Tables** from the left-hand column.

6. Select **Weather Observation Table.** Here you will see the data you entered for all your daily observations in a single table.

7. If you would prefer to develop your own database, see the "Designing an Access Database" section in Project AC-01.

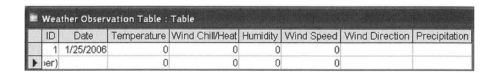

For more information online, go to:

http://atm.geo.nsf.gov/instruction/observations.html

THE CONTINENTS

Project Number: AC-06

Additional hardware: None

Internet connection required? Yes

Template available? Yes

Grade Level: Elementary, Middle School, High School

2
Easy

Created by:
Student

Project type:
Instructional

Student learning style:
Visual

Approximate time: 30 minutes to create a seven-continent table

Content Area:
Social Studies

Comments: A major component of many social studies curriculums is the study of the seven continents. Microsoft Access can be an especially useful tool in these studies, as students collect and analyze information in their research.

Procedures:

1. From the companion CD, open Microsoft Access Project AC-06, The Continents.

2. From the left-hand column, select **Forms**.

3. Open the Continents Form. This will give you a form for entering information about each of the world's continents.

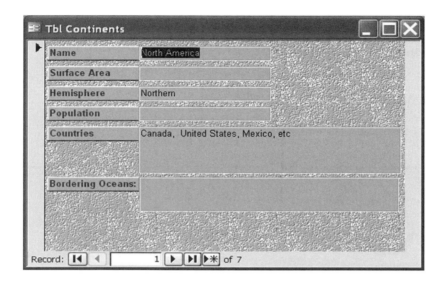

4. Enter data on the form, including the continent name, total surface area, location hemisphere, population, major countries located on that continent, and bordering oceans.

5. To see the information in table format, minimize the Continent Form and select **Tables** from the left-hand column.

6. Select **Continent Table.** Here you will see the data you entered for all your continents in a single table.

7. By selecting **Records > Filter > Advanced Filter Sort**, you can realign your data table in other ways that might make it easier to see relationships between the attributes. You may want to order the continents by size, population, or location. Sorting and grouping using different attributes can reinforce the learning process.

8. If you would prefer to develop your own database, see the "Designing an Access Database" section in Project AC-01.

For more information online, go to:

http://www.enchantedlearning.com/geography/continents/

PLANETS

Project Number: AC-07

Additional hardware: None

Internet connection required?   Yes

Template available?   No

Grade Level: Elementary, Middle School, High School

Created by:

Student

Project type:

Instructional

Student learning style:

Visual

Approximate time: 45 minutes to create a nine-planet database

Content Area:

Science

Comments: Students are often fascinated by outer space. State learning and content standards require students to learn about the planets that make up our solar system. Microsoft Access provides a simple way to record significant data about each of the planets and then sort the data by any of the desired attributes. This database is well suited to group work, where different students research one or more of the planets, then pool their information into a single database.

Procedures:

1. From the companion CD, open Microsoft Access Project AC-07, Planets.

2. From the left-hand column, select **Forms.**

3. Open the Planets Form. This will give you a form for entering information about each of the known planets in the solar system.

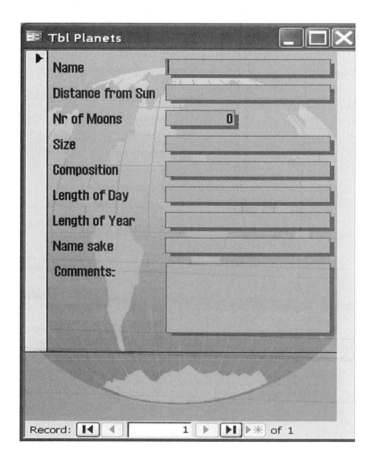

4. Enter data on the form, including planet's name, distance from the sun, number of moons, size, composition, length of day, length of year, mythological namesake, and any additional comments.

5. To see the information in table format, minimize the Planets Form and select **Tables** from the left-hand column of the window.

6. **Select Planets Table.** Here you will see the data you entered for all your planets in a single table in **Design View.**

Access

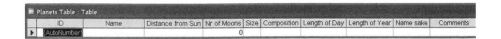

ID	Name	Distance from Sun	Nr of Moons	Size	Composition	Length of Day	Length of Year	Name sake	Comments
(AutoNumber)			0						

7. To reorder the appearance of the planets in the database, select **Records** from the drop-down menus available at the top of the screen. **Select Filter > Advanced Filter Sort**.

8. Click in the **Field** cell in the first column. Click on the drop-down arrow that appears on the right side of the cell.

9. Select the desired attribute field from the options on the drop-down menu. Return to the **Filter** drop-down menu and select **Apply Filter Sort,** and the database should recalibrate and update itself in accordance with your selected criteria.

10. If you would prefer to develop your own database, see the "Designing an Access Database" section in Project AC-01.

For more information online, go to:

http://www.nineplanets.org/

CLASS LIBRARY

Project Number: AC-08

Additional hardware: None

Internet connection required? No

Template available? Yes

Grade Level: Elementary, Middle School, High School

2
Easy

Created by:
Student and/or Teacher

Project type:
Administrative

Student learning style: N/A
Not Applicable

Approximate time: 15 minutes to catalog 10 books

Content Area:
Language Arts

Comments: What classroom is complete without books? Whether just a few or shelves and shelves of them, chances are you may find yourself in need of an easy way to keep track of the books in your collection. Microsoft Access can be used to design forms and tables to simplify your record keeping. You can enter the information into the database yourself or have your students do it as part of a group project.

Access

Procedures:

1. From the companion CD, open Microsoft Access Project AC-08, Class Library.

2. From the left-hand column, select **Forms.**

3. Open the Class Library Form. This will give you a form for entering information about each of the books in your collection.

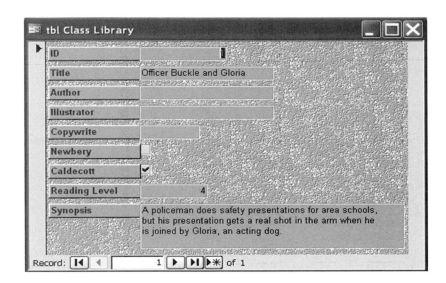

4. Enter data on the form, including book title, author, illustrator, copyright date, reading grade level, and a brief synopsis of the story. Additionally, there are boxes to check if the book is a Newbery or Caldecott Award winner. The entry for Officer Buckle and Gloria has been partially completed by way of example.

5. To see the information in table format, minimize the Class Library Form and select **Tables** from the left-hand column.

6. Select **Class Library Table.** Here you will see the data you entered for all your books in a single table.

7. If you would prefer to develop your own database, see the "Designing an Access Database" section in Project AC-01.

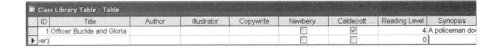

For more information online, go to:

http://teacher.scholastic.com/reading/bestspractices/classlibraries.htm

GEOMETRIC SHAPES

3

Medium Difficulty

Project Number: AC-09

Additional hardware: None

Internet connection required?   No

Template available?   Yes

Grade Level: Elementary, Middle School, High School

Created by:
Student and/or
Teacher

Project type:
Instructional

Student learning style:
Visual

Kinesthetic

Approximate time: 30 minutes to create a 10-shape set

Content Area:
Math

Comments: Many students struggle with the study of geometry. Confusion may exist between the various shapes in terms of definitions, shape, and other attributes. Using Microsoft Access, you can create a database that will allow your students to see the differences between the different shapes while at the same time noting the principle attributes of each.

Access

Procedures:

1. From the companion CD, open Microsoft Access Project AC-09, Geometric Shapes.

2. From the left-hand column, select **Forms**.

3. Open the Geometric Shapes Form. This will give you a form for entering information about each of the geometric shapes.

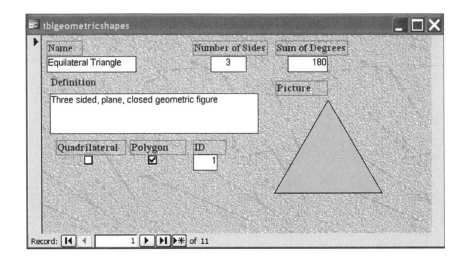

4. Enter data on the form, including shape name, number of sides, sum of internal degrees, definition of the shape, boxes to check for quadrilaterals and polygons, and a graphic representation of the geometric shape. Forms have been partially completed for several shapes by way of example.

5. To see the information in table format, minimize the Geometric Shapes Form and select **Tables** from the left-hand column.

6. Select **Geometric Shapes Table.** Here you will see the information you entered for the various geometric shapes in one table. By selecting **Records > Filter > Advanced Filter Sort**, you can realign your data table in other ways that might make it easier to see relationships between the attributes.

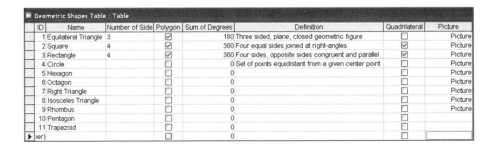

7. Additionally, the companion CD has a PowerPoint slide labeled "Fifteen Geometric Shapes" that contains images of all these shapes and several more. Simply open the PowerPoint slide, copy the desired image, and paste it into the correct spot on a blank form.

8. This project could be used as an assessment tool. For younger students, the teacher could provide a series of images on the forms and have students list the other characteristics. Older students could be asked to write the definitions of the indicated shapes.

9. If you would prefer to develop your own database, see the "Designing an Access Database" section in Project AC-01.

For more information online, go to:

http://42explore.com/geomet.htm

VIDEO LIST

Project Number: AC-10

Additional hardware: None

Internet connection required?   No

Template available?   Yes

Grade Level: Elementary, Middle School, High School

3

Medium Difficulty

Created by:

Teacher

Project type:

Administrative

Student learning style: N/A

Not Applicable

Approximate time: 30 minutes to create a 10-video listing

Content Area: N/A

Not Applicable

Comments: Microsoft Access is a database management system that can truly revolutionize the way you keep records in your classroom. Several features of Access help make this a versatile program that allows customized input and output formats. For this project, you will develop a database that will allow you to record and catalog your collection of classroom videos. You will develop a simple form to fill out that is linked to a database. You can then sort the database by any criteria you select (title, subject, date, etc.).

Procedures:

1. From the companion CD, open Microsoft Access Project AC-10, Video List.

2. From the left-hand column, select **Forms**.

3. Open the Video List Form. This will give you a form for entering information about each of your videos.

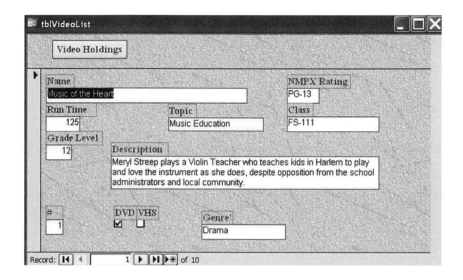

4. Enter data on the form, including video name, NMPX rating, run time, topic, class, grade level, description, entry number, and genre. Check either the DVD or VHS block. Several sample entries have been included by way of example.

5. To see the information in table format, minimize the Video List Form and select **Tables** from the left-hand column.

6. Select Video Table. Here you will see the data you entered for all your videos in a single table.

#	Name	Genre'	NMPX Rating	Run Time	Topic	Class	Grade Level	Description	DVD	VHS
1	Music of the Heart	Drama	PG-13	125	Music Education	FS-111	12	Meryl Streep plays a Violin Teacher who teaches kids in Harlem to play and love the instrument as she does, despite opposition from the school administrators and local community.	☑	☐
2	Emperor's Club, The	Drama	PG-13	123	Integrity, Honor	FS-111	12	At an annual Competition about Greek history, a student wins by cheating. Twenty years later, he demands a rematch to clear his name - and he cheats again. The "Win at all Cost" mentality costs him his wife and family, but he is without	☑	☐
3	Dead Poets Society	Drama	PG-13	121	Education	FS-111	12	Robin Williams, an English teacher at an exclusive boys' school, revives an ancient club, The Dead Poets Society, where the students are encouraged to become independent thinkers.	☑	☐
4	Stand and Deliver	Drama	PG-13	122	Math Education	Teacher Education	12	Jamie Escalante, a teacher at a Bario school, helps kids get ahead in life by teaching them Advanced Placement Calculus	☑	☐
5	Paper Chase	Drama	PG-13	135	Education	FS-111	12	Students at Harvard Law School achieve against all odds. Starring John Houseman	☑	☐
6	To Sir, With Love	Drama	PG	118	Education	FS-111	12	Sidney Portier stars as a teacher in England who helps kids grow up and develop respect for the teacher in the process	☑	☐
7	Goodbye, Mr. Chips	Drama	G	125	Education	FS-111	12	Mr. Chips, a teacher at an all boys school becomes headmaster during WW-II. He teaches generations of students as they transition from boys to men	☑	☐

Access

Additionally, the form has a command button placed near the top. Open the Video List Form and click on the button labeled **Video Holdings**. This will create a report showing the title, NMPX rating, run time, and description of all videos in the database.

Video List

Name	NMPX Rating	Run Time	Description
Dead Poets Society	PG-13	121	Robin Williams, an English teacher at an exclusive boys' school, revives an ancient club, The Dead Poets Society, where the students are encouraged to become independent thinkers.
Emperor's Club, The	PG-13	123	At an annual Competition about Greek history, a student wins by cheating. Twenty years later, he demands a rematch to clear his name - and he cheats again. The "win at all cost" mentality costs him his wife and family, but he is without remorse.
Goodbye, Mr. Chips	G	125	Mr. Chips, a teacher at an all boys' school becomes headmaster during WW-II. He teaches generations of students as they transition from boys to men.
Miracle Worker, The	G	122	Anne Sullivan, a young teacher, is assigned to a young deaf-blind girl named Hellen Keller.

For more information online, go to:

http://www.wbra.org/html/edserv/ntti/nttipdf/02media.pdf

STUDENT DATA

3

Medium Difficulty

Project Number:	AC-11
Additional hardware:	None
Internet connection required?	No
Template available?	Yes
Grade Level:	Elementary, Middle School, High School

Created by:

Teacher

Project type:

Administrative

Student learning style: **N/A**

Not Applicable

Approximate time: 30 minutes to create 10 student records

Content Area:

Language Arts

Math

Science

Social Studies

Comments: As a teacher, you may have occasional need to contact your students outside of regular class hours. Whether to send a get well card to one who is sick, call a parent to discuss student behavior, or invite family members to attend a class function, a student directory could prove invaluable. Microsoft Access makes it easy to design a template to support your record-keeping needs.

Access

Procedures:

1. From the companion CD, open Microsoft Access Project AC-11, Student Data.

2. From the left-hand column, select **Forms**.

3. Open the Student Data Form. This will give you a form for entering information about each of your students.

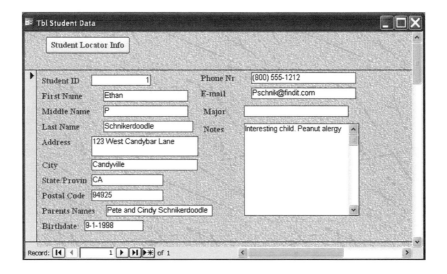

4. Enter data on the form, including student's name, address, parent/guardian names, e-mail address, major, general notes, and birth date.

5. To see the information in table format, minimize the Student Data Form and select **Tables** from the left-hand column.

6. Select **Student Data Table.** Here you will see the data you entered for all your students in a single table. The data in this table can be sorted as needed to rearrange the order of display.

7. Additionally, the form has a command button placed near the top. Return to the **Forms** view and click on the button labeled **Student Locator Info**. This button is linked to the Reports function of Access. This will create a summary report showing the contact information and birth date of each of your students.

8. If you would prefer to develop your own database, see the "Designing an Access Database" section in Project AC-01.

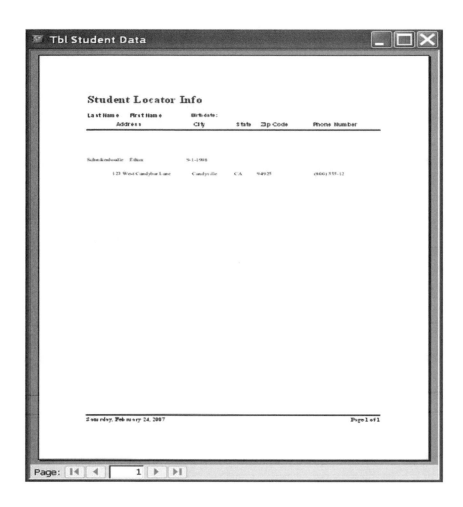

For more information online, go to:

http://office.microsoft.com/en-au/templates/TC010184071033.aspx

Clouds

Project Number:	AC-12
Additional hardware:	None
Internet connection required?	No
Template available?	None
Grade Level:	Elementary, Middle School, High School

3

Medium Difficulty

Created by:

Student

Project type:

Instructional

Student learning style:

Visual

Approximate time: 30 minutes to create a five-cloud database

Content Area:

Science

Comments: Children are often fascinated by clouds. Ask a group of students to gaze up, and you will get as many interpretations of the cloud formations as you have students. State academic standards often require that students be able to recognize the various cloud types. In science class, student will learn how to distinguish among the various cloud types by their features. For related projects, see PP-09, Weather Report; XL-01, Recording Weather; or AC-05, Weather Observations.

Access

Procedures:

1. From the companion CD, open Microsoft Access Project AC-12, Clouds.

2. From the left-hand column, select **Forms**.

3. Open the Cloud Form. This will give you a form for entering information about each of the various cloud types.

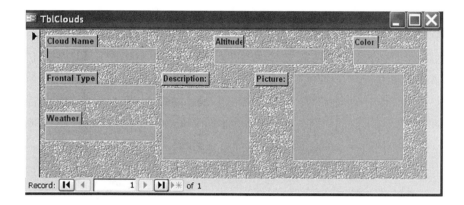

4. Enter data on the form, including cloud name, height, color, associated frontal type, a description of the cloud, and the type of weather a particular cloud heralds. Additionally, there is a space on the form where you can cut and paste images of the cloud under consideration.

5. To see the information in table format, minimize the Cloud Form and select **Tables** from the left-hand column.

6. Select **Cloud Table.** Here you will see the data you entered for all your clouds in a single table.

7. If you would prefer to develop your own database, see the "Designing an Access Database" section in Project AC-01.

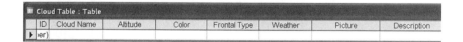

For more information online, go to:

http://vortex.plymouth.edu/cloudboutique/

STUDENT BEHAVIOR

Project Number:	AC-13
Additional hardware:	None
Internet connection required?	No
Template available?	Yes
Grade Level:	Elementary, Middle School, High School

3

Medium Difficulty

Created by:

Student and/or Teacher

Project type:

Administrative

Student learning style: N/A

Not Applicable

Approximate time: 10 minutes to create one-day documentation

Content Area:

Language Arts

Math

Science

Social Studies

Comments: Documenting student behavior is an important element of any good classroom management plan. If you have a student who seems to be in need of special education services to succeed academically, you will need to produce documentation to support your concern. Additionally, records of student behavior can prove useful to child study teams, special education committees, IEP committees, and parent-teacher conferences. Microsoft Access provides a simple way to track student behavior and look for patterns.

Higher-functioning students may find this project useful as a tool for self-monitoring of improper behavior. By having the student document his or her own infractions, the student may prove more receptive to suggestions for improvement.

Procedures:

1. From the companion CD, open Microsoft Access Project AC-13, Student Behavior.

2. From the left-hand column, select **Forms**.

3. Open the Student Behavior Form. This will give you a form for entering data on the behavior of designated students.

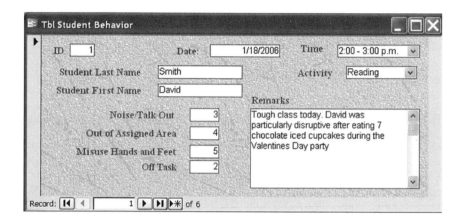

4. Enter data on the form, including date, time, activity, specific behavior infractions, and general remarks. Data for observations on David Smith have been completed by way of example.

5. To see the information in table format, minimize the Student Behavior Form and select **Tables** from the left-hand column.

6. Select **Student Behavior Table.** Here you will see the data you entered for all your Student Behavior in a single table.

7. If you would prefer to develop your own database, see the "Designing an Access Database" section in Project AC-01.

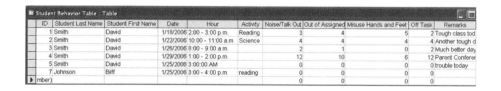

For more information online, go to:

http://cecp.air.org/fba/problembehavior3/reinforcement3.htm

PEER REVIEW

Project Number: AC-14

Additional hardware: None

Internet connection required? No

Template available? Yes

Grade Level: Elementary, Middle School, High School

4

Difficult

Created by:
Student and/or
Teacher

Project type:
Administrative   Instructional

Student learning style:
Visual

Aural

Approximate time: 60 minutes to create a single peer review

Content Area:
Language Arts   Science

Social Studies

Comments: One way to encourage your students to work to the best of their abilities is to use a peer review process when grading written assignments. Peer grading using a rubric has several advantages. Students who know the specific grading criteria for each portion of an assignment are better prepared to meet those standards. Having students grade each other's work may introduce an element of fairness to the process. Additionally, students may develop an appreciation for the strengths and weaknesses of their own writing by critically evaluating the individual components of work submitted by peers. Using Microsoft Access, you can create an interactive scoring rubric that computes total scores based on individual selections.

Procedures:

1. From the companion CD, open Microsoft Access Project AC-14, Peer Review.

2. From the left-hand column, select **Forms**.

3. Open the Peer Review Form. This will give you a form for entering data for the peer review.

4. For the sample rubric given, graders will rate the assignment based on the following criteria:
   Topic sentence
   Supporting details
   Vocabulary
   Grammar and spelling
   Capitalization and punctuation
   Conclusion

5. Each of these criteria can be individually rated on a scale of 5 to 1, as follows:
   5 = Outstanding
   4 = Excellent
   3 = Good
   2 = Fair
   1 = Poor

This particular rubric has a scoring range of from 6 to 30 points total.

6. The sum total of individual scores will appear in the upper right corner of the rubric, in the Overall Score box.

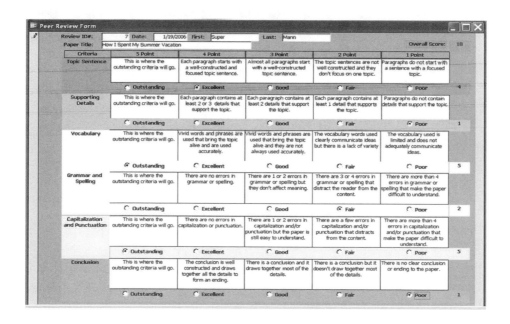

7. You can tailor the information in any of the description boxes to fit your unique needs and specific grading criteria. To do so, select **View** from the drop-down menu at the top of your screen. Select **Design View** from the available options.

8. Click on any of the data boxes on the form to change the wording as desired.

9. Save your work by selecting **File > Save.**

10. To return to the form, select **View > Form View.**

11. Advance to the next record using the forward arrow of the record number field at the lower left corner of the form.

12. To view a table with all the evaluations for a particular student, minimize the Peer Review Form. Select **Tables > Peer Review Tab**. This will show a table with all peer evaluations conducted to date. These data can then be sorted as desired, depending on the intended use.

13. If you would prefer to develop your own database, see the "Designing an Access Database" section in Project AC-01.

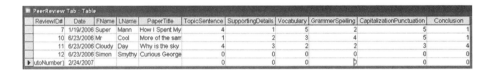

For more information online, go to:

http://writing.colostate.edu/guides/teaching/peer/

NOTES

6

Microsoft Publisher Projects

In this chapter you will find the following activities:

Project Number	Title	Difficulty	Created By
PL-01	Signs	1	Student and/or Teacher
PL-02	Student Resume	1	Student
PL-03	Award Certificate	1	Student
PL-04	Information Flyer	1	Student
PL-05	Special Events Sets	1	Student and/or Teacher
PL-06	Homework Pass	1	Teacher
PL-07	Homework Calendar	1	Student and/or Teacher
PL-08	Bookplate Labels	1	Student and/or Teacher
PL-09	Letterhead Stationery	1	Student and/or Teacher
PL-10	Postcard	1	Student and/or Teacher
PL-11	Concert Program	2	Student and/or Teacher
PL-12	Yearbook or Program Ads	2	Student and/or Teacher
PL-13	Class Newsletter	2	Student and/or Teacher
PL-14	Information Brochure	2	Student
PL-15	Greeting Cards	2	Student
PL-16	Banner	2	Student and/or Teacher
PL-17	Tent Card	2	Student and/or Teacher
PL-18	Poster	2	Student and/or Teacher
PL-19	Business Cards	2	Student
PL-20	Class Web Site	4	Student

INTRODUCTION TO MICROSOFT PUBLISHER

Brochures, flyers, newsletters, posters, banners—these are just a few of the items you can create using Microsoft Office Publisher. All these and more can be easily created and printed on your computer's printer. This is an application known as desktop publishing. Quite simply, this program allows you to publish all manner of printed media from the ease and comfort of your personal computer. Although some of these items can also be created using Microsoft Word, you will soon find that the added features of Publisher will make it your preferred application for print media.

There are many similarities between Microsoft Word and Microsoft Publisher, and for this reason, many folks may feel no need to learn a new program when they may already be quite comfortable with Word. After all, teachers have been creating newsletters, signs, greeting cards, and many other projects for several years now using standard Word software. However, once you try Publisher and see how much better suited it is for certain applications, you may be hard-pressed to remain with Word. There are differences between the two, and some applications are better suited for one than for the other. For instance, due to its precise control in positioning and manipulating text with images, Microsoft Publisher is better suited for the following projects: Graphically rich print and e-mail newsletters, catalogs, greeting cards, posters and banners, three- or four-panel brochures or flyers, business cards, and design materials to be commercially printed. On the other hand, due to the extensive word-processing capabilities of Microsoft Word, it is better suited for the following kinds of projects: Documents with a table of contents and index; long documents, such as research papers or business plans, or legal documents; short documents that can make use of templates and wizards, and documents that are to be reviewed and edited by others.

Unfortunately, Publisher can run only on Windows-based programs. Many people who do lots of graphic work in high-end commercial print shops prefer to work with Apple computers and must therefore use a different application. Still, despite these facts, Microsoft Publisher is a fine, entry-level, desktop publishing program, more than adequate for most classroom usage. Additionally, Microsoft Publisher is not included in some collections of Microsoft Office programs. Microsoft Publisher in 2000 came only as part of the Professional Edition, so not every classroom computer will have Publisher installed. If you are running an older version, you probably will not be able to do many of these Publisher projects. Collections may include only Word, PowerPoint, Excel, and Access as part of the package, so be sure to check before you buy.

From bulletin board accents to letters to parents to room decorations or even labels for posted class artwork, the easy-to-use wizards in Microsoft Publisher allow you to create professional-looking print media without having to run to the corner copy center. You can even use Publisher to design and post a Web page for your class or school. This book contains 20 different products you can make in class, simply by using the sample provided on the companion CD or by generating them from scratch with the user-friendly Microsoft Publisher wizards. Sample projects include award certificates, information flyers, homework passes, postcards, student resumes, greeting cards, bookplate labels, and business cards, to name a few.

Unlike the other chapters in this book, the Microsoft Publisher projects described here make almost exclusive use of the templates that come with the program. With hundreds of preplanned project schemes available, you are sure to find existing projects that will prove quite useful in the classroom. Still, this is not meant to stifle individual creativity as much as to stimulate it.

Publisher

SIGNS

Project Number:	PL-01
Additional hardware:	Printer
Internet connection required?	No
Template available?	None
Grade Level:	Elementary, Middle School, High School

Very Easy

Created by:
Student and/or
Teacher

Project type:
Administrative

Instructional

Student learning style:

Visual

Approximate time: 10 minutes to create a sign

Content Area:
Language Arts

Math

Science

Social Studies

Comments: Signs can serve many purposes in a school building. They can be used to give direction, welcome guests, identify classes, and warn of danger. Sign making is arguably one of the easiest projects in this collection, and Microsoft Publisher has many templates that can easily accommodate all your signage needs.

Publisher

Procedures:

1. Open Microsoft Publisher.

2. Select **Publications for Print > Signs**.

3. Pick a template from the 40 available.

4. Add text, and insert graphics if desired.

5. To insert a graphic image you have saved, select **Insert > Picture > From File.** Navigate to where the desired graphic is stored, select the image, and click **Insert**. To adjust the size and location of the image, move the cursor over one of the image "handles" and click and drag to the desired size. Drag the entire image to the desired location.

6. Print and laminate your sign, if desired.

For more information go to Microsoft Publisher Help and search for *signs*.

STUDENT RESUME

1
Very Easy

Project Number:	PL-02
Additional hardware:	Printer
Internet connection required?	No
Template available?	Yes
Grade Level:	Middle School, High School

Created by:
Student

Project type:
Instructional

Student learning style:
Visual

Approximate time: 45 minutes to create one student resume

Content Area:
Not Applicable

Comments: One way to determine if we have been successful as teachers is if our students are able to get a job after they leave the classroom. A key document in many job hunts is the resume. Even students who are too young for paid employment can find value in going through the steps needed to create a resume. Additionally, since federal special education laws require students with disabilities to have postschool transition plans, a resume may be an important component to that plan. Microsoft Publisher has several resume templates that can help streamline the writing process for your students.

Publisher

Procedures:

1. Open Microsoft Publisher.

2. Select **Publications for Print > Resumes > Entry Level**.

3. Select a design from among the several offered.

4. Enter the information requested in the spaces indicated on the template, including objective, education, awards, work experience, volunteer work, and references.

Print and distribute to potential employers.

Biff Skipperdoodle

Objective
A job where I can use my skills as a friendly person and a hard worker to best advantage.

Education
Budville Middle School
Buddville High School 10th grade

Awards
Honor Roll
Principal's List
Varsity Baseball Team
Varsity Track Team

Work Experience
200X—200X Pet Care Specialist
Self Employed
Walked dogs for 8 families while they were on summer vacation

200X—200X Lawn Case
Self Employed
Mowed 5 Lawns each week in local housing development

200X—200X Lead Me Alone
Self Employed
Raked leaves for residents of local community

Volunteer Work
Helped serve meals at the homeless shelter
Library beautification project—Pick up trash around Library
as an Eagle Scout Project

References
Neil Armstrong, Scoutmaster, 555-1234
Billy Graham—pastor, 777-7777

For more information go to Microsoft Publisher Help and search for *resume.*

AWARD CERTIFICATE

1
Very Easy

Project Number: PL-03

Additional hardware: Printer

Internet connection required? No

Template available? Yes

Grade Level: Elementary, Middle School, High School

Created by:
Student

Project type:
Administrative

Student learning style:
Visual

Approximate time: 15 minutes to create one certificate

Content Area:
Language Arts

Math

Science

Social Studies

Comments: There are almost as many ways to motivate students as there are students. Some are motivated to do well as a result of extrinsic rewards; others are more intrinsically motivated. Using Microsoft Publisher, you can create all manner of award certificates to recognize your students for stellar behavior or for demonstrating a desired skill level in a given area. You may want to create individualized awards for all your students for presentation at an end-of-year activity.

Publisher

Procedures:

1. Open Microsoft Publisher.

2. From the drop-down menu, select **Publications for Print > Award Certificates.**

3. Select a desired template from the several dozen offered.

4. Type in your desired message, inserting graphics as desired.

5. Print and distribute. What could be easier?

For more information online, go to:

http://office.microsoft.com/en-ca/assistance/HP030763891033.aspx

INFORMATION FLYER

Very Easy

Project Number:	PL-04
Additional hardware:	Printer
Internet connection required?	No
Template available?	Yes
Grade Level:	Elementary, Middle School, High School

Created by:
Student

Project type:
Administrative

Student learning style:
Visual

Approximate time: 30 minutes to create one flyer

Content Area:
Language Arts

Math

Science

Social Studies

Comments: Information exchange is a key element in any well-run classroom. It is important to keep parents and students informed of upcoming events and activities if you are to expect their support of these activities. Microsoft Publisher has dozens of built-in templates to help you create beautiful and informative flyers as part of your classroom communication plan. You can create flyers to inform parents of upcoming parent-teacher conferences, open house night, or facts about an upcoming field trip. You could incorporate flyers into student lessons or have your students develop promotional materials describing a scientific discovery or historical event.

Procedures:

1. Open Microsoft Publisher.

2. From the drop-down menu, select **Publications for Print > Flyers > Informational.**

3. Select a desired template from the several dozen offered.

4. Type in your desired message, inserting graphics as desired.

5. Print and distribute. What could be easier?

For more information online, go to:

http://office.microsoft.com/en-us/assistance/ha010348591033.aspx

SPECIAL EVENTS SETS

Very Easy

Project Number:	PL-05
Additional hardware:	Printer
Internet connection required?	No
Template available?	Yes
Grade Level:	Elementary, Middle School, High School

Created by:
Student and/or
Teacher

Project type:
Administrative

Student learning style: N/A
Not Applicable

Approximate time: 45 minutes to create a special events set

Content Area:
Language Arts

Math

Science

Social Studies

Comments: On occasion, you may be involved with planning, publicizing, and executing a large event of some sort. Perhaps you're in charge of the annual spring carnival, science fair, or field day. You may want to develop several different types of printed material in support of the event—publicity flyers, postcards, banners, name tags, registration materials, posters, award certificates, and program brochures. Students can help develop these promotional materials. With Microsoft Publisher special event sets, you can choose a common theme that will appear in all your printed materials, giving a more professional appearance to your efforts.

Procedures:

1. Open Microsoft Publisher.

2. Select **Design Sets > Special Event Sets**, and choose from the collections offered.

3. Individually select the desired components (flyer, brochure, etc.).

4. Enter the desired information in the spaces provided on the templates.

5. Save the documents in a file until needed.

6. The special event set with the "Blackboard" theme is shown here.

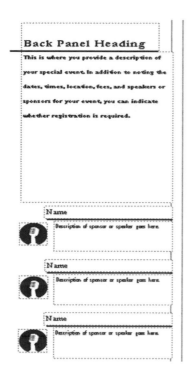

For more information go to Microsoft Publisher Help and search for *design sets*.

HOMEWORK PASS

1

Very Easy

Project Number: PL-06

Additional hardware: Printer

Internet connection required? No

Template available? Yes

Grade Level: Elementary, Middle School, High School

Created by:

Teacher

Project type:

Administrative

Student learning style: N/A

Not Applicable

Approximate time: 15 minutes to create one homework pass

Content Area:

Language Arts

Math

Science

Social Studies

Comments: Of all the incentives teachers can give their students in the bid to elicit desired behavior, the homework pass may well prove to be one of the most effective. Microsoft Publisher contains several gift certificate templates that can be readily adapted to the much-coveted homework pass.

Procedures:

1. Open Microsoft Publisher.

2. Select **Publications for Print > Gift Certificates.**

3. Under gift certificate options, choose a publication design from the more than 30 templates offered.

4. Select color and font schemes, or stay with the default values if desired.

5. Fill in the necessary identifying information.

6. Determine the required number of copies per sheet and select **One** or **Multiple**.

7. Print and distribute your homework passes to students who earn them.

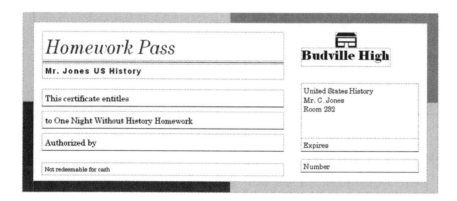

For more information online, go to:

http://office.microsoft.com/en-au/assistance/HA011264391033.aspx

HOMEWORK CALENDAR

1

Very Easy

Project Number: PL-07

Additional hardware: Printer

Internet connection required? No

Template available? Yes

Grade Level: Elementary, Middle School, High School

Created by:

Student and/or
Teacher

Project type:

Administrative

Student learning style: N/A

Not Applicable

Approximate time: 20 minutes to create a one-week calendar

Content Area:

Language Arts

Math

Science

Social Studies

Comments: One of the more daunting administrative tasks of running a classroom is the management of homework assignments. Microsoft Publisher can help make this chore easier. By using the calendar features of this program, you can create a document that will help students track what assignments are due and when. If you are an advance planner and know what you intend to teach for the entire month and the supporting homework to go along with those lessons, list them on a calendar and give to the students at the beginning of each month. If you prefer a more flexible homework policy, leave blank spaces for the student to record his or her own assignments on a daily basis.

Procedures:

1. Open a Microsoft Publisher document.

2. Select **Publications for Print > Calendars > Full Page.**

3. Choose from the approximately 60 available templates.

4. Select **Change date range** to choose a specific month and year for your homework calendar.

5. Enter title and identifying information as needed.

6. Enter either a) homework information for the entire month or b) just the subject titles and allow the students to enter specific assignment information.

7. Print and distribute.

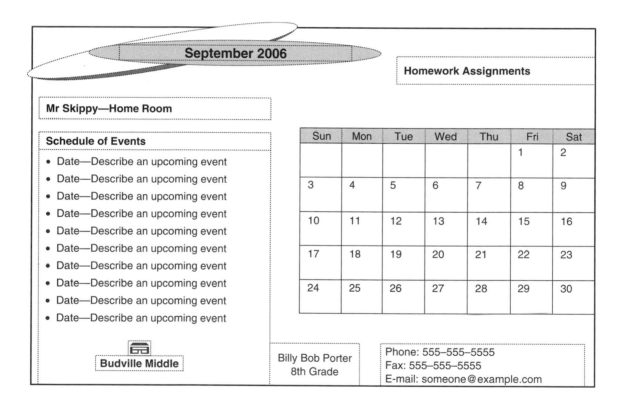

For more information go to Microsoft Publisher Help and search for *calendar*.

BOOKPLATE LABELS

Project Number: PL-08

Additional hardware: Printer

Internet connection required? No

Template available? Yes

Grade Level: Elementary, Middle School, High School

1
Very Easy

Created by:
Student and/or
Teacher

Project type:
Administrative

Student learning style: **N/A**
Not Applicable

Approximate time: 10 minutes to create a bookplate label

Content Area:
Language Arts

Comments: The typical classroom may hold dozens, if not hundreds of books available for students to read. Teachers may purchase additional materials for their own professional development or for leisure reading, and may occasionally loan these books out to peers or students. It will be easier for your loaned book to find its way back to your library if you place some identifying name on the inside cover. Additionally, student-made books will take on an added look of smartness if they are properly labeled. Microsoft Publisher has several bookplate label templates from which to choose.

Procedures:

1. Open a Microsoft Publisher document.

2. Select Publications for **Print > Labels > Bookplates**.

3. Choose one of the available designs.

4. Add your name in the space provided. If desired, replace the image with one of your own choosing.

5. The template labels are sized to fit on pregummed Avery labels. The particular label you need will be determined by the individual template you choose. If you prefer, you can print your labels on plain paper, cut them out, and glue them into the books as needed.

6. Print the labels according to the directions of your specific printer.

For more information online, go to:

http://www.rif.org/readingplanet/activitylab/color.mspx

LETTERHEAD STATIONERY

1

Very Easy

Project Number: PL-09

Additional hardware: Printer

Internet connection required? No

Template available? Yes

Grade Level: Elementary, Middle School, High School

Created by:
Student and/or
Teacher

Project type:

Administrative

Instructional

Student learning style:
Visual

Approximate time: 10 minutes to create letterhead stationery

Content Area:
Language Arts

Math

Science

Social Studies

Comments: Good teachers communicate—with students, parents, faculty, staff, and others—often using written notes. What better way to add a personal touch to your written correspondence than with letterhead stationery? Microsoft Publisher has templates that will allow you to create beautiful personalized stationery with a few clicks of the mouse and a few words of text. Perfect for sending notes to parents or thanking a student for those homemade Christmas cookies.

Procedures:

1. Open Microsoft Publisher.

2. Select **Publications for Print > Letterhead > Plain Paper.**

3. Choose one of the more than 50 templates available, or design your own.

4. Insert your own information as desired in the spaces provided on the template.

5. For letters that will be sent to groups of people, you may want to type your message directly onto the letterhead stationery. Additionally, you may want to print some blank sheets of stationery for handwritten notes.

For more information go to Microsoft Publisher Help and search for *letterhead.*

POSTCARD

1

Very Easy

Project Number: PL-10

Additional hardware: Printer

Internet connection required? No

Template available? Yes

Grade Level: Elementary, Middle School, High School

Created by:

Student and/or Teacher

Project type:

Administrative

Instructional

Student learning style:

Visual

Approximate time: 15 minutes to create one postcard

Content Area:

Language Arts

Math

Science

Social Studies

Comments: Another great tool that Microsoft Publisher provides is a series of templates for making postcards. Postcards can be used to introduce yourself at the beginning of the school year or to notify parents of special events at the school. Students can create postcards to send to pen pals at sister schools in other states or countries.

Publisher

Procedures:

1. Open Microsoft Publisher.

2. Select **Publications for Print > Postcards**, and select from the options indicated. For this example, we will select **Informational**.

3. Choose a template from the more than 40 options available.

4. Select the appropriate size and number of copies per sheet you want to have.

5. Fill in the blanks as desired, and add graphics if you like.

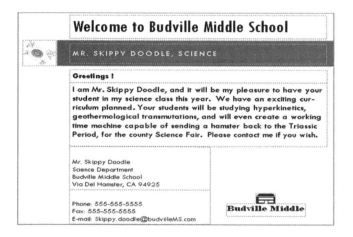

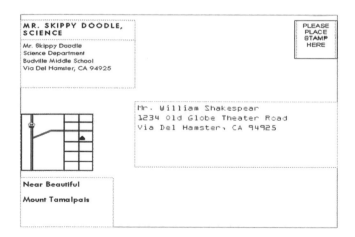

For more information go to Microsoft Publisher Help and search for *postcard.*

CONCERT PROGRAM

1
Very Easy

Project Number: PL-11

Additional hardware: Printer

Internet connection required? No

Template available? Yes

Grade Level: Elementary, Middle School, High School

Created by:
Student and/or
Teacher

Project type:
Administrative

Student learning style: N/A
Not Applicable

Approximate time: 30 minutes to create a single concert program

Content Area:
Language Arts

Math

Science

Social Studies

Comments: Programs! Programs! Get your programs here! Can't tell the players without a program! Microsoft Publisher makes it easy to create professional-looking programs for all your special events. You can make programs for music concerts, drama productions, or sporting events. The template provided is for a four-page program, but you can modify it to suit your needs.

Procedures:

1. Open Microsoft Publisher.

2. Select **Publications for Print > Programs**, and choose from the available designs. The **Music** design is used here.

3. Fill in the desired information on the front cover by clicking on the individual text boxes.

4. Edit the inside pages by clicking on the page indicator near the bottom of the screen, shown here:

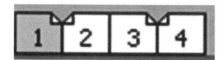

5. Continue to edit inside pages until program is complete.

For more information go to Microsoft Publisher Help and search for *programs.*

YEARBOOK OR PROGRAM ADS

1

Very Easy

Project Number: PL-12

Additional hardware: Printer

Internet connection required? Yes

Template available? Yes

Grade Level: Elementary, Middle School, High School

Created by:

Student and/or Teacher

Project type:

Administrative

Student learning style: **N/A**

Not Applicable

Approximate time: 30 minutes to create a full-page ad

Content Area:

Language Arts

Comments: Microsoft Publisher has many uses at school in addition to those that are strictly academic in nature. Teachers are sometimes called on to serve as advisers for clubs and committees, not the least challenging of which is the group tasked with producing the annual school yearbook. Microsoft Publisher has templates that will simplify the process of composing advertisements found in such publications. With Publisher, you or your students can quickly produce professional-looking, copy-ready ads for yearbooks or sponsors of special programs.

Publisher

Procedures:

1. Open Microsoft Publisher.

2. From the drop-down menu, select **Publications for Print > Advertisements**.

3. Select a desired template from those offered.

4. Type in the information desired by the sponsor of the advertisement, inserting text and graphics as required.

5. Decide on logo, size of ad, and copies per sheet (full page, half page, quarter page, or eighth page).

6. Print and submit for publication.

For more information go to Microsoft Publisher Help and search for *advertisements.*

CLASS NEWSLETTER

1

Very Easy

Project Number: PL-13

Additional hardware: None

Internet connection required? No

Template available? Yes

Grade Level: Elementary, Middle School, High School

Created by:
Student and/or
Teacher

Project type:
Instructional

Student learning style:
Visual

Approximate time: 45 minutes to create a two-page newsletter

Content Area:
Language Arts

Science

Social Studies

Comments: Class newsletters can be used for several things in the classroom. They can be either student-generated or teacher-generated and can be used to assess student progress, entertain classmates, and inform parents of classroom activities.

Procedures:

1. Open a new Microsoft Publisher document.

2. Select Publications for **Print > Newsletters**.

3. Microsoft Publisher has an excellent menu-driven process with many design templates, lay-outs, and color schemes to choose from.

4. The number of pages should be in multiples of two. While the default value for a newsletter is generally four pages, you can add or delete pages as desired.

5. To add pages, select **Insert > Page** from the drop-down menu.

6. To reduce the number of pages, highlight the desired page number in the lower left corner of the screen, select **Edit** from the drop-down menu, then **Delete Page**. If your newsletter is set up for two-sided printing, you will get a box with choices to delete Both Pages, Left Side Only, or Right Side Only. Select the desired option.

7. To highlight just one page, you may need to first select "one-sided printing" from the Newsletter Options task pane.

8. Your newsletter can Include many of the following items:
   a. Letter of introduction
   b. Class rules
   c. Homework policy
   d. Parent volunteers
   e. Schedule of events
   f. Homework coupon
   g. Announcements
   h. Supply list
   i. Introduction of the curriculum

9. A sample newsletter may look similar to the following:

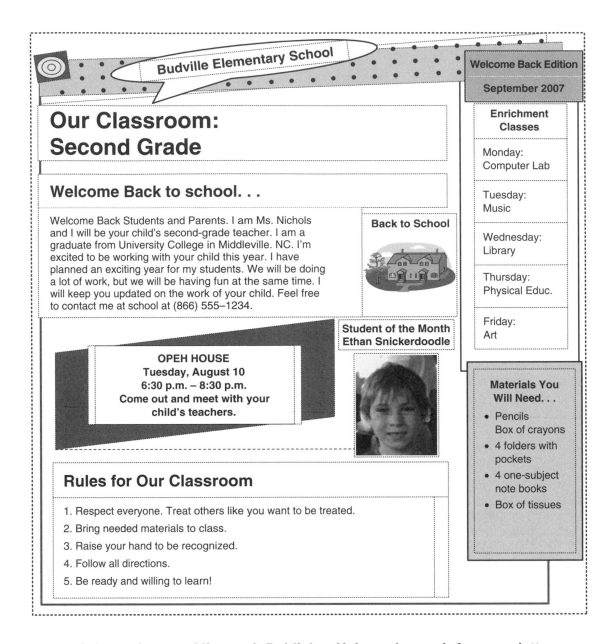

For more information see Microsoft Publisher Help and search for *newsletter*.

Thanks to Amy Nichols for her original version of the sample Project PL-13.

INFORMATION BROCHURE

1

Very Easy

Project Number:	PL-14
Additional hardware:	Printer
Internet connection required?	No
Template available?	Yes
Grade Level:	Elementary, Middle School, High School

Created by:

Student

Project type:

Instructional

Student learning style:

Visual

Approximate time: 60 minutes to create a brochure

Content Area:

Language Arts

Math

Science

Social Studies

Comments: The information brochure is an excellent product for assessing student knowledge about a subject. Students can create these on any number of topics in any discipline area. They can create "travel brochures" for a country they've studied or perhaps a brochure describing life as a soldier in the Civil War. Brochures could be used to explain the generation and uses of electricity or perhaps as a way to show what a student has learned about the Roman Empire or even as a way to present experimental data. This method may also prove useful for determining the academic progress of students with disabilities where portfolio assessment may be appropriate.

Procedures:

1. Open Microsoft Publisher.

2. Select **Publications for Print > Brochures > Informational.**

3. Select one of the design templates available (Office 2003 has over 60 designs from which to choose), or create your own from scratch.

4. Fill in the information as desired in the predesignated blocks.

5. Insert clipart or other graphics as needed.

6. Save the document and print. Remember that you will need to print on both sides of the page, so you may have to experiment with your specific printer to get the orientation correct on the back side.

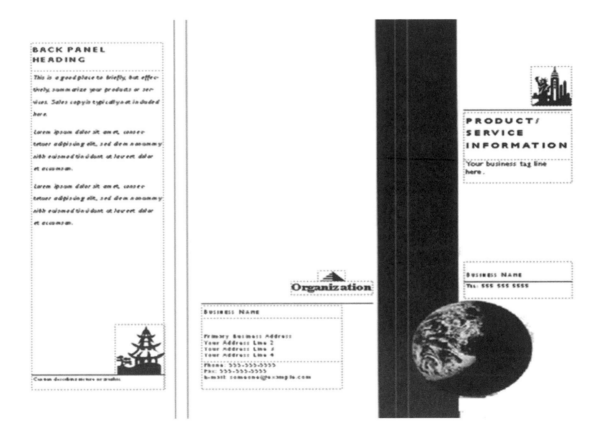

MAIN INSIDE HEADING

The most important information is included here on the inside panels. Use these panels to introduce your organization and describe specific products or services. This text should be brief and should entice the reader to want to know more about the product or service.

You can use secondary headings to organize your text to make it more scannable for the reader.

Lorem ipsum dolor sit amet, consectetuer adipiscing elit, sed diem nonummy nibh euismod tincidunt ut lacreet

Lorem ipsum dolor sit amet, consectetuer iusto odio dignissim qui may nibh euismod tincidunt ut lacreet dolore magna aliguam erat volutpat.

Custom description picture or graphic.

SECONDARY HEADING

Lorem ipsum dolor sit amet, consectetuer adipiscing elit, sed diem nonummy nibh euismod tincidunt ut lacreet dolore magna aliguam erat volutpat. Ut wisi enim ad minim veniam, consequat, vel illum dolore eu frugiat nulla facilisis at vero eros et accumsan et iusto odio dignissim qui blandit praesent luptatum. Lorem ipsum dolor sit amet, consectetuer adipiscing elit, sed diem nonummy nibh euismod tincidunt ut lacreet dolore magna aliguam erat volutpat. Ut wisi enim ad minim veniam, consequat, vel illum dolore eu frugiat nulla facilisis at vero eros et accumsan.

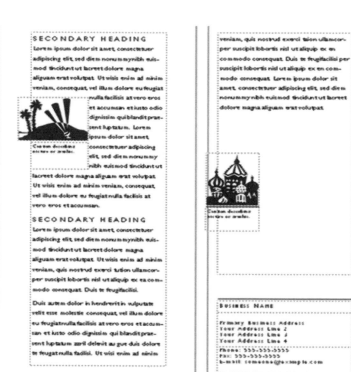

Custom description picture or graphic.

SECONDARY HEADING

Lorem ipsum dolor sit amet, consectetuer adipiscing elit, sed diem nonummy nibh euismod tincidunt ut lacreet dolore magna aliguam erat volutpat. Ut wisi enim ad minim veniam, quis nostrud exerci tution ullamcorper suscipit lobortis nisl ut aliquip ex ea commodo consequat. Duis te frugifacilisi.

Duis autem dolor in hendrerit in vulputate velit esse molestie consequat, vel illum dolore eu frugiatnulla facilisis at vero eros et accumsan et iusto odio dignissim qui blandit praesent luptatum zzril delenit au gue duis dolore te frugait nulla fadilisi. Ut wisi enim ad minim

veniam, quis nostrud exerci tution ullamcorper suscipit lobortis nisl ut aliquip ex en commodo consequat. Duis te frugifacilisi per suscipit lobortis nisl ut aliquip ex en commodo consequat. Lorem ipsum dolor sit amet, consectetuer adipiscing elit, sed diem nonummy nibh euismod tincidunt ut lacreet dolore magna aliguam erat volutpat.

Custom description picture or graphic.

BUSINESS NAME

Primary Business Address
Your Address Line 2
Your Address Line 3
Your Address Line 4
Phone: 555-555-5555
Fax: 555-555-5555
E-mail: someone@example.com

For more information online, go to:

http://www.microsoft.com/education/persuasionbrochure.mspx

GREETING CARDS

Very Easy

Project Number:	PL-15
Additional hardware:	Printer
Internet connection required?	No
Template available?	Yes
Grade Level:	Elementary, Middle School, High School

Created by:
Student

Project type:
Instructional

Student learning style:
Visual

Kinesthetic

Approximate time: 20 minutes to create a greeting card

Content Area:
Not Applicable

Comments: Throughout the school year, there may be occasions when you want your students to write a greeting card of some sort. What mother or grandmother wouldn't appreciate a card from her student on her special day? Or perhaps a sympathy card for a student who has lost a close friend, relative, or a cherished pet or a get-well card during a prolonged illness. Valentine's Day presents numerous opportunities for card exchanges. Creating greeting cards could be integrated into an existing social skills development program for students needing help in this area.

Publisher

Procedures:

1. Open Microsoft Publisher.

2. Select **Publications for Print > Greeting Cards.**

3. Select the particular type of card desired (Thank You, Birthday, Mother's Day, etc.).

4. Preview the available card templates and select one. Microsoft Office has more than 300 templates from which to choose.

5. Fill in the desired information, and insert additional clipart or photos if you like. Be sure to add stuff to all four pages (front, inside front, inside back, and back). Change pages by clicking on the page numbers located near the bottom left corner of the screen.

6. The inside of your completed card may look something like this:

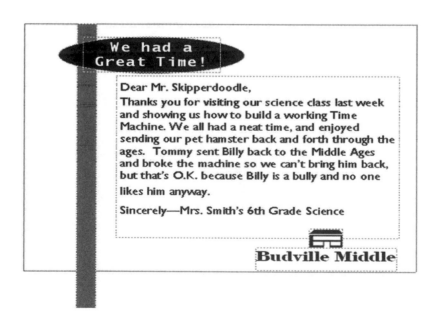

For more information see Microsoft Publisher Help and search for *greeting cards.*

Publisher

BANNER

Project Number: PL-16

Additional hardware: Printer

Internet connection required? No

Template available? Yes

Grade Level: Elementary, Middle School, High School

Created by: Student and/or Teacher

Project type:

 Administrative

 Instructional

Student learning style: Visual

Approximate time: 10 minutes to create one banner

Content Area:

 Language Arts

 Math

 Science

 Social Studies

Comments: There are dozens of possible uses for banners in your classroom and school. Banners can help welcome students back to school, welcome parents to open house night, add spirit to a pep rally, acknowledge teacher appreciation week, promote a new display of reference materials in the school library, or identify projects for the science fair. The possibilities are limited only by your imagination.

Procedures:

1. Open Microsoft Publisher.

2. Click on **Publications for Print > Banners**. Select the desired type of banner from the list presented. For this example, we will select **Welcome**, then the **Welcome Back** banner.

3. Next, choose the width and height you want the banner to be. The height will be determined by whether you prefer portrait or landscape orientation of the individual sheets of paper that will make up your banner.

4. Determine placement of graphics, if any, and select a border option.

5. Your banner will print using multiple pages, the number depending on the banner length you chose. Print the pages and attach them together.

For more information go to Microsoft Publisher Help and search for _banner._

TENT CARD

2
Easy

Project Number:	PL-17
Additional hardware:	Printer
Internet connection required?	No
Template available?	Yes
Grade Level:	Elementary, Middle School, High School

Created by:
Student and/or
Teacher

Project type:
Administrative

Student learning style: N/A
Not Applicable

Approximate time: 15 minutes to create a tent card

Content Area:
Language Arts   Science   Social Studies

Comments: At some time in your teaching career you may be charged with designing name placards to designate seating at a conference or banquet table. Or perhaps you need a free-standing name card identifying a display at a science fair or open house. The Microsoft Publisher Tent Card is well suited for these purposes.

Procedures:

1. Open Microsoft Publisher.

2. Select **Blank Publications > Tent Card.**

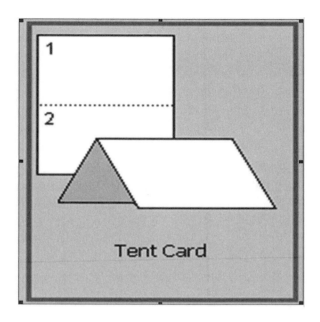

3. A window will open, asking if you want to automatically insert a second page in your publication. Click **Yes** if you want information to appear on both sides of the folded tent card. Otherwise, select **No**.

4. To add text, select **Insert > Text Box**, from the drop-down menu near the top of the screen.

5. Click and drag a text box where you want the text to be. Remember that since the card will be folded, the surface area on the screen represents only half the final page. You can fill the screen with text or images if you like, and it will still cover only the bottom half of the final product. If you prefer landscape orientation rather than the default portrait orientation, select **File > Page Setup > Landscape** orientation. Adjust font size and options as needed.

6. To insert graphics, follow the procedures listed in Project PL-01, Step 5.

7. Add your text.

8. If this is to be free-standing, print your tent card on heavy-duty card stock, fold, and display.

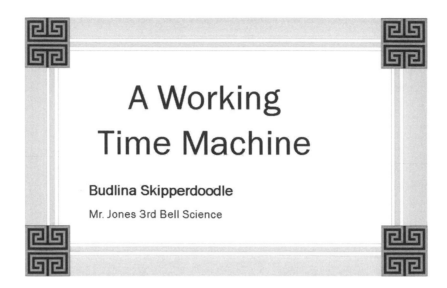

For more information go to Microsoft Publisher Help and search for *table tent*.

NOTES

POSTER

Project Number:	PL-18
Additional hardware:	Printer
Internet connection required?	No
Template available?	Yes
Grade Level:	Elementary, Middle School, High School

2 Easy

Created by:
Student and/or Teacher

Project type:
Administrative · Instructional

Student learning style:
Visual

Approximate time: 30 minutes to create a poster

Content Area:
Language Arts · Math · Science · Social Studies

Comments: Posters can be used to inform, educate, entertain, or decorate. What classroom would be complete without posters adorning the walls? Students may create posters as part of their assigned projects. Posters can be used as a part of your classroom management plan, listing class rules or level markers for each student. They can also display key information for your students, such as the class schedule or the week's spelling words. Microsoft Publisher allows you to create posters of varying size and dimension, according to need. These posters will be printed on multiple pages then assembled to create a single poster.

Procedures:

1. Open Microsoft Publisher.

2. Select **Blank Publications > Poster.**

3. To add text, select **Insert > Text Box** from the drop-down menu near the top of the screen.

4. Click and drag a text box where you want the text to be. Adjust font size and options as needed.

5. Add your desired text.

6. To add pictures or graphics, select **Insert > Picture** from the drop-down menu near the top of the screen.

7. Go to **File > Page Setup**, and select the desired size of the final poster.

8. Print, assemble the individual sheets, and laminate the entire poster if desired.

Class Rules

1. Keep Hands and Feet to Self
2. Raise Hand to Speak
3. Remain in Your Area.
4. Respect Others

For more information see Microsoft Publisher Help and search for *poster.*

BUSINESS CARDS

Project Number: PL-19

Additional hardware: Printer

Internet connection required? No

Template available? Yes

Grade Level: Elementary, Middle School, High School

2
Easy

Created by:

Student

Project type:

Instructional

Student learning style:

Visual

Approximate time: 15 minutes to create a business card

Content Area:

Language Arts

Comments: As students get older, they may develop an interest in earning money. Many students go into business for themselves, walking dogs, mowing lawns, or raking leaves. And what business is complete without a business card? With Microsoft Publisher, your students can create professional-looking business cards to give to prospective clients or employers.

Procedures:

1. Open Microsoft Publisher.

2. Select **Publications for Print > Business Cards.**

3. Select a template from the more than 50 designs available.

4. Enter text, contact information, and graphics as needed in the spaces provided.

5. Select a logo (if desired), orientation, and copies per sheet, as needed.

6. Print your completed cards on heavy-duty cardstock, or on perforated sheets specially designed for business cards. These are available at most office supply stores.

For more information go to Microsoft Publisher Help and search for *business cards*.

CLASS WEB SITE

4
Difficult

Project Number:	PL-20
Additional hardware:	None
Internet connection required?	Yes
Template available?	Yes
Grade Level:	Middle School, High School

Created by:

Student

Project type:

Instructional

Student learning style:

Visual

Kinesthetic

Approximate time: 120 minutes to create an eight-page Web site

Content Area:

Language Arts

Comments: A class Web site can be used to meet a variety of classroom management needs. It can be used to inform parents and community of class-sponsored activities, classroom homework and discipline policies, upcoming events, and other things. Used as an interactive tool, it can even be used to take orders for fundraising items such as T-shirts and candy, solicit parent feedback, and collect survey data. Additionally, the technology standards required by most school districts require students to demonstrate the ability to create Web sites.

This can be done as a student project or teacher created for the entire school or for the classroom. You can even create Web sites for student-run businesses.

Publisher

Procedures:

1. Open a new Microsoft Publisher document.

2. Select **Web Sites and E-Mail** and select the types and number of pages desired from the available menu.

3. Microsoft Publisher has an excellent menu-driven process with many design templates, layouts, and color schemes to choose from.

   Examples of pages you may want to create include these:
   a. Information page, describing the class
   b. Contact information for the teacher
   c. Special offers for school emblematics or other sale items
   d. Calendar of school activities
   e. Links to other Web sites
   f. Samples of student artwork or written assignments
   g. Letter of introduction
   h. Class rules
   i. Homework policy
   j. Parent volunteers
   k. Schedule of events
   l. Homework coupon
   m. Announcements
   n. Supply list
   o. Introduction of the curriculum

4. You may choose to post your Web site as a link to the school or district Web site. See your school or school district technology specialist for directions on how to do this.

For more information online, go to:

http://www.busyteacherscafe.com/webpage_tutorial.htm

Thanks to Crystal Gunn for her original version of the sample Project PL-20.

Index